Hartwood

BRIGHT,
WILD FLAVORS
FROM THE
EDGE OF THE
YUCATÁN

Hartwood

ERIC WERNER   MYA HENRY

WITH CHRISTINE MUHLKE AND OLIVER STRAND
PHOTOGRAPHS BY GENTL & HYERS
FOREWORD BY RENÉ REDZEPI

ARTISAN
NEW YORK

Library of Congress Cataloging-in-Publication Data

Werner, Eric.
    Hartwood / Eric Werner and Mya Henry, with
Christine Muhlke and Oliver Strand ; foreword by
René Redzepi ; photographs by Gentl & Hyers.
        pages cm
    Includes bibliographical references and index.
    ISBN 978-1-57965-620-1 (alk. paper)
    1. Cooking, Mexican. 2. Maya cooking. 3. Hartwood
(Restaurant : Tulum, Mexico) I. Title.
    TX716.M4W47 2015
    641.5972—dc23
                                    2015013061

Design by Michelle Ishay-Cohen
Map by Emily Isabella

Artisan books are available at special discounts
when purchased in bulk for premiums and
sales promotions as well as for fund-raising
or educational use. Special editions or book
excerpts also can be created to specification.
For details, contact the Special Sales Director
at the address below, or send an e-mail to
specialmarkets@workman.com.

Published by Artisan
A division of Workman Publishing Company, Inc.
225 Varick Street
New York, NY 10014-4381
artisanbooks.com

Published simultaneously in Canada by
Thomas Allen & Son, Limited.

Printed in China

First printing, September 2015

10 9 8 7 6 5 4 3 2 1

To the forever
inspiring Maya community
and to Mexico's Yucatán
Peninsula, *Dios bo'otik*.

Hartwood

JICAMA SALAD
EMPANADAS DE PAPAYA
ENSALADA DE TOMATE MILPA
YUCATAN CEVICHE
ENSALADA DE PESCADO AHUMADO
GRILLED MAYAN PRAWNS

FILETE DE CORONADO
COSTILLAS AL AGAVE
ARRACHERA ANGUS
FILETE DE ROBALO
COSTILLAR DE RES
PLATILLO DE PULPO
PESCA DEL DIA
SIDES-BEET/CAMOTE/PLATANO

Contents

FOREWORD BY RENÉ REDZEPI

Every year right after Christmas, when Copenhagen is about to be at its bleakest, I tap out. My wife and I wrangle our three little daughters and set out on the twenty-hour odyssey to Mexico. When we get there, we like to spend most of our time in the Yucatán, as close to the water as possible.

During those two or three weeks, the kids spend the days crawling all over us, I tackle the reading list that has grown on my desk throughout the fall, and I wear flip-flops again. For someone in my trade, it's as close as you can get to normal. And it always works out for us: we focus on one another and I undergo the necessary reboot for the grueling months that await me back in Denmark: new year, new interns, new menu.

The people, the beaches, that rare feeling of being allowed to disconnect—it's more than enough to make the journey worthwhile. But recently it has become clear that the reason we want to add more days to the Tulum leg of our trip is the restaurant Hartwood.

When you go to Eric and Mya's place, you're right in the jungle. There's no roof, no walls, just a little bit of electricity. At dusk and into the starry night, the space transmits an energy that's difficult to describe: Desmond Dekker plays on the sound system, and cocktails of mezcal mixed with fresh-squeezed juices keep coming your way. We'd be happy going there again and again just to sit on one of those benches and take it all in.

But once a whole grouper arrives at the table and everyone starts attacking it like they haven't seen food in days, you realize that you're there to eat. Then Eric sends out a watermelon salad—exactly what you were craving at that moment, even though you didn't know it—followed by a simmering cauldron of beef cooked with honey and plates of beets, octopus, and other offerings from the area, all perfectly cooked over the embers.

I am a mega-fan of Mexican cuisine. I love tasting the layers of history in the food. But what Eric cooks doesn't taste Mexican. This is despite the fact that Hartwood is as local as local gets: Eric spearfishes for his seafood and visits markets in town, where families sell produce grown right beside their homes. Farmers in the middle of nowhere are the lifeline of the restaurant.

The cooking is singular and addictive—the reason people line up for hours every day to eat there, even though their vacation time is precious. When I've been working so hard I can't tell if it's day or night, and I know I need to take a break even though I don't have the time, this is the place I dream about.

I'm sure Eric and Mya didn't imagine it when they first hung that little sign in front of the restaurant, but they ended up making food you can't get anywhere else and transforming the area in the process. It makes me happy and a bit jealous when I think about the fact that they did all this by leaving the big city and finding their own path.

Tokyo, January 2015

THE YUCATÁN: COME FIND US

MEXICO

GULF OF MEXICO

MEXICO

The Yucatán Peninsula is at the southeast corner of Mexico, a flat mass of land just south of the Tropic of Cancer, with the Gulf of Mexico to one side and the Caribbean to the other. When you fly over the Yucatán, all you see is a thick carpet of green. At first it might seem like you're looking at field or pasture, but it's jungle, and it's so dense you can't see through the canopy to the ground below.

Three states make up the Yucatán Peninsula: Campeche, Yucatán, and Quintana Roo. Hartwood is in Tulum, a small town in Quintana Roo that's a ninety-minute drive south from Cancún, the now-intense resort area that was created in 1970 on what was then a desolate beach. The shoreline to the south of Cancún is known as the Riviera Maya, a tourist-bureau name for one of the most beautiful coastlines anywhere: white sand, teal water, palm trees. When you think of the perfect image of a Caribbean beach, you're thinking of the Riviera Maya.

The Riviera Maya gets its name from the Mayas who still live here. For many in the region, Spanish is a second language—Yucatec Maya is spoken at home. Tulum is a modern town built inland from a Maya temple complex that dates to the fifth century. Almost everything here can be measured on one of two timelines, one ancient and the other just a few decades old.

Development of the beach zone in Tulum didn't begin until the 1980s. A ten-minute drive from town, the beach still doesn't have power lines or telephone service. Until recently, the only tourists were international beach bums or yoga fanatics staying at hotels that were little more than shacks of lashed-together branches with thatched palm roofs.

A single road runs along the water, and it wasn't paved until a decade ago. On one side are the beach and the beach hotels, which are now more than shacks but are still low, simple buildings that are easy to put back together after a storm. On the other side is the jungle. That's where you'll find us.

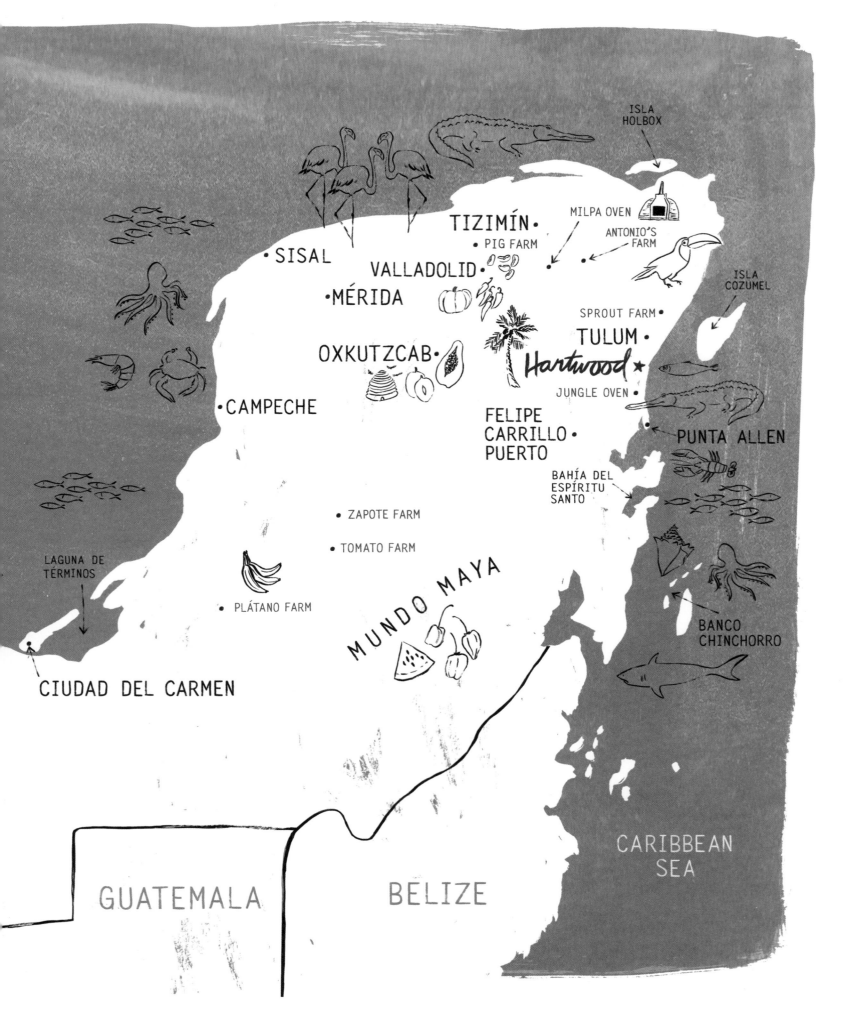

ISLA
HOLBOX

TIZIMÍN ·

· PIG FARM

MILPA OVEN

ANTONIO'S
FARM

· SISAL

VALLADOLID

· MÉRIDA

ISLA
COZUMEL

SPROUT FARM ·

TULUM ·
Hartwood ★

OXKUTZCAB ·

JUNGLE OVEN

· CAMPECHE

FELIPE
CARRILLO ·
PUERTO

PUNTA ALLEN

BAHÍA DEL
ESPÍRITU
SANTO

· ZAPOTE FARM

· TOMATO FARM

BANCO
CHINCHORRO

LAGUNA DE
TÉRMINOS

· PLÁTANO FARM

MUNDO MAYA

CIUDAD DEL CARMEN

CARIBBEAN
SEA

GUATEMALA   BELIZE

It Began

In December 2009, we found ourselves at the one stoplight in Tulum, wondering what would happen if we didn't make that right turn toward the airport. For the last few days of our escape from freezing New York City, we'd been fantasizing about starting a new life here. What would our lives be like if we didn't have to work until 2 a.m. every morning and weren't always worried about paying rent? There were restaurants in Tulum, but there was room for more, and everyone in town seemed to know how to relax. When they worked, they worked hard, but when they had time to themselves, they spent it drinking up this paradise. We could picture swimming in the clear blue Caribbean in the morning, cooking in the evening, and closing up to travel during the summer.

Sometimes you dream out loud because it feels good to put voice to a fantasy, then you go back to your old habits. But the more we talked, the more we began to realize that we were serious about staying. Maybe. What if we changed our tickets, told everybody back home that the flights were canceled, and spent a few days crunching numbers and looking at real estate? What if we changed our lives entirely?

At the time, the only commitment we had was to each other. We didn't have kids. We didn't own property. We had jobs we could leave. We knew we were fortunate to have work following the financial collapse the year before, but we were so caught up with the high-RPM restaurant world that we never had time to see each other.

We'd begun asking ourselves what it was all for. Then, finally, one day, we decided it was time to give up a rent-stabilized East Village apartment, pack up our lives, and move to Tulum.

We returned to Mexico in May 2010. We had only a vague plan at that point. We were still looking at properties and just beginning to untangle the complicated regulations that governed the real estate on the beach. It's a protected environment, and it's literally off the grid—the power lines stop at the bend in the road. We weren't interested in taking over an existing restaurant. We wanted to build one ourselves—even if that meant installing a septic system and having potable water trucked in every day. If we wanted electricity, we'd have to look to solar panels and gas generators, so we decided that the restaurant would cook everything on wood, either on a grill or in an oven—no propane burners or electric rings. That meant finding a supply of properly cured hardwood in a part of the world where the jungle is so lush and humid that dead trees don't dry out—they're eventually reabsorbed by the land.

In July, we found a place: an unappreciated, overgrown piece of the jungle right on the beach road with a fig tree out front. The plot was about 3,000 square feet, and it sloped steeply. The palm trees and plants were so thick you couldn't see the ground. We fell in love with it.

We could afford it because of the money we had saved, the possessions we'd eBayed, and Mya's good credit rating. At the time, there wasn't much on the jungle side of the road. All the hotels and most of the restaurants were on the beach side, facing the water. There were a handful of restaurants and shops on the jungle side, but it was generally ignored, more of a place for a hotel to locate a generator or a parking area. But it was within our budget. And, from the front, you could catch glimpses of the beach, though you could hear the water better than you could see it.

We signed the papers in August.

When we'd first started talking about doing this, everyone looked at us like we were crazy. It was just the two of us, but it finally began to happen. The permits were filed and approved and we started to clear the land. We didn't have a crew of workers or a backhoe; we had ourselves and some machetes.

As we hacked though the plants, we came across snakes and iguanas and other creatures. There was standing water in places, and you could sink into the mud up to your thighs. It was certainly culture shock from what we knew in New York, not because of the overwhelming sense of being out in nature, but because we were moving so slowly after living in a city where everything is boom–boom–boom. We were forced to realize our approach was totally wrong and we needed to relax a little bit.

That's when we first learned the double meaning of *mañana*. It can mean two things: it can mean "tomorrow," or it can mean, "Yeah, later, like tomorrow or something." When you're told, "*Mañana, mañana,*" you're actually going to get it tomorrow morning. If you need it right away, it's better to hear the *mañana, mañana* rather than just the *mañana*. Because when you get just the *mañana*, well, you never know when that will be. It could be sometime tomorrow, or never. Or it could mean, "Next week when I feel like it, or when I need money again, because right now I don't need money, so, yeah, *mañana*." Both *mañana, mañana* and *mañana* serve their purpose. You just need to know when you need which one.

We were working with a team of talented young architects who were hungry to get a start in Tulum. At first they wanted something more streamlined and modern, but we wanted a place that looked frozen in time, as if settlers had just tied up their boat and unloaded all of their possessions, their battered metal teapots and silverware and linen napkins. We wanted it to feel like a shipwreck. And we wanted it to be open to the sky and to the road and to the jungle.

All of our hard work is what drew people to Hartwood, especially in the beginning, when it was so simple and we were really just right out in the open for everybody to see. We were sweating. We made mistakes. But people were kind. In an era of huge, well-financed restaurants, they saw what was going on and said, "This is a love project, isn't it?"

It still is.

Cenotes provide respite from the heat when the ocean can't cool you off. There is nothing that compares to its crisp, mineral-rich water. Cenotes are home to turtles, fish, tropical birds, and—from time to time—a crocodile or two.

THE
OPEN
KITCHEN

When we built the restaurant, we decided to keep most of it open to the sky. That wasn't the plan at first, but as we started clearing the land, we realized that the sky was an important part of why we loved it there. One night there were so many stars that we stopped working to look up. There was nothing we could build that would be as beautiful as the night.

The downside is that when it rains hard, we have to close. Sometimes we know when the rain is going to come, and we don't open that day. But other times we're caught off guard, the entire staff standing under the roof in the kitchen looking out onto an empty restaurant. The truth is, we'll take it. The magic of serving food to a "room" of people sitting under the stars is worth the risk of the occasional rainout.

The restaurant has two and a half walls. One wall is the back of the kitchen, where we built the grill and wood–burning oven, and the other wall separates our property from our neighbor. The wall in the front of the restaurant is a half wall you can easily step over. We wanted to be open to the activity outside: vendors and tourists on beach cruisers during the day, taxis and people dressed for dinner and carrying flashlights at night. After we close, the night porters hang their hammocks, keep watch over Hartwood, and discourage visitors.

There are no power lines here, but we have a simple though effective system of solar panels and a gas generator to replenish the batteries so that the freezer stays cold and the sound system stays on. The fact is, we could use lots of power and run the generator all night, but we chose not to do that because when you come here, we want you to talk to your friends and feel the breeze float in off the jungle.

Sky, stars, and the glow of the oven at the edge of the jungle—these are the foundation of the Hartwood experience.

Hard work and all our hearts went into building the kitchen at Hartwood. Once we set foot on our little piece of land, we never left. Whether or not the restaurant is open, we're in the kitchen every day.

We string together
gardenias on jute twine
and then hang them
from meat hooks. Beauty
and fragility juxtaposed
with a certain rawness
is how Hartwood could
be described.

The smell of roasted and burning wood is in our skin and a part of us. It adds depth to the food we serve and makes each bite more flavorful. But to smell and taste smoke is a gift. Our daughter agrees.

THE
YUCATÁN
SEASONS

Spring, summer, fall, and winter don't mean much in Tulum. Instead, there's high season, which starts with the winter holidays, when tourists from the United States and Europe fill the hotels and pack the beaches. The craziest stretch is from Christmas Eve through New Year's, when it seems as if all of New York City has flown down to go for a swim. It's exciting to feel the rise of that buzzy energy, but the beach road is jammed with traffic all day long, and we're so busy we don't have time to see any of our friends who came down. High season peaks again on Valentine's Day and during the midwinter school break in February, then ends after Semana Santa, the holy week that follows Easter Sunday.

Almost all of the businesses here make most of their money during the high season. That means there's an explosion of activity in October and November, when Tulum is overtaken by a mad rush of construction. New restaurants appear out of nowhere, old restaurants grow second floors, all the walls get a fresh coat of paint. The work is done then because there won't be time to stop and fix anything until April.

Then there is the rainy season. The wet weeks start in late June and end in October. Because we're on the sea, we do get freak storms during the dry season, and dry stretches when it should be wet, but we usually know when the rains will come. In July, an extreme heat settles in that doesn't leave until early October.

Hartwood is closed in September: between the heat and the rains, there's no point in staying open, so we use the time to work on the restaurant. Maintenance is essential in this environment, and this is the time for us to do the big jobs (fix the roof, refurbish the septic system) we can't do when we're open.

But when it comes to produce, the season is never-ending. Something is always just coming into the markets in this abundant region. Every day there is produce at its peak.

THE HARTWOOD WAY

At Hartwood, we start a lot of our dishes on the grill and finish them in the wood-burning oven. The grill gives you nice markings and a subtle wood flavor so that the food has a foundation of char and smoke, while the oven cooks it quickly and thoroughly. It's not so different from how most professional kitchens work: there you start with a sauté pan on the burner, then finish by putting it in a hot oven. We're doing the same thing, only the fuel we use is wood.

At home, most people don't have a grill and a wood-burning oven. But you have other options, and what you do is up to you. You could cook the food entirely on the grill: Start over a high-heat, high-flame zone and then move to a medium-hot part of the grill, where it will cook through without being incinerated. You could grill over wood, then complete the dish in a preheated conventional oven. Or if you don't have a grill, turn up the burner on your range: use a well-oiled cast-iron skillet brought to a high temperature on a burner so that it gives what you're cooking a nice sear, then transfer the pan to a hot oven.

Clockwise from top left: Avocado leaves, whole mamey, dried jamaica (hibiscus) flowers, cinnamon bark, plátanos, and mamey cut in half.

HOW TO COOK WITH WOOD

We don't choose to work over open flames because we're fire junkies who need to prove ourselves by how hot we can get our oven. We do it to be in a silent conversation with the fire. It's amazing that something can be so quiet and yet so powerful. No two fires are ever the same. The fire is like the sea or the wind, a force of nature that you can direct but that you can't fully control. You build it, tend to it. Then you follow it.

The best way to understand how to cook with wood fire is through practice. Experience is the best teacher, and you'll learn more from your mistakes than when everything goes as planned. That said, there are a few tricks you can get from this book.

One, roast the wood before putting it on the fire: Place two or three pieces of wood at a time on a grill grate set well above the kindling so that the flames dry out the wood even more than it is already. (Make sure that the grate is high enough that the wood won't catch—it's okay if a few splinters flame up, but you don't want to start a second fire.) If you roast logs before adding them to the fire, they will ignite in seconds, not minutes.

Two, use a four-inch stub of candle to help start the fire. (At Hartwood, we use the ends from the candles from the dining room.) Crumple up two or three sheets of newspaper, pile the kindling on top, and put the candle deep in the center of your construction—it's the nucleus. When you light the newspapers, the fat from the candle will act as an accelerant, and the candle will fuel the fire.

Three, use the roasted wood to build a structure that will allow the air to come in and feed the flames. You want the air to enter through the bottom, so stack the wood to create an opening that functions like a door. Put light, dry wood on the bottom and denser wood on top. The light wood will catch more easily and then ignite the denser wood, which will burn into a bed of embers. That's what you want. You can use the high flames of a catching fire to heat up pans and boil water, but you want to cook over low flames or embers. High flames will scorch the outside of what you're cooking and leave the inside raw; the rolling flames you get from the embers will give you a good surface sear and cook the food all the way through.

The flames are what make grilling with wood different from grilling with lump charcoal or briquettes—that and the flavor they impart, which is smokier and cleaner. You can learn to control the flames. It's not so different from cooking on the stovetop, where you turn the burner knob to increase the heat. Add wood to bring up the temperature and create more flames: If you add two pieces, it's similar to giving a quarter-turn to the knob; four pieces it's a half-turn. If you want to bring the heat down, use your tongs to move some of the wood to the side.

When you're cooking a piece of meat, you want high heat, with intense flames, to add grill marks and to sear the exterior. You don't want fat-fed flare-ups, but the high heat is important. It should be uncomfortably hot—if you can hold your hand close to the grill, there isn't enough heat to cook a steak or a piece of lamb.

It's different when you're cooking fish. You want high heat at first to crisp up the skin so that it doesn't stick to the grill, but then you want to bring down the heat quickly so that the flesh cooks evenly. If you add pieces of wood to sear the skin, you may want to move them to the side to cook the fish the rest of the way, then repeat for the other side. This isn't a hard-and-fast rule, though. It could be that the wood you're using produces intense flames, or it could be that it burns down and becomes part of the bed of embers. You're not going to learn how to grill over wood from a cookbook, you're going to learn by doing. You need to watch the flames, the wood, the food. You need to make mistakes. You will get better, but it will take time.

Eusebio brings us top-cut wood, dried out by the sun, to fuel our fires.

THE WOOD-BURNING OVEN

A wood-burning oven is another beast. Each oven has its own personality, and it takes time to understand the particular characteristics of how it works. As you get to know your oven, you'll see that it doesn't have a uniform temperature. There are hot spots, more stable pockets, areas where the flame licks along the ceiling and curls down toward the floor. Every time you use it, it's an education. Test the limits of your oven within reason, and test yourself. Try everything: meat, fish, vegetables, bread, cakes. Once you start on this path, your approach to cooking will change forever.

The oven at Hartwood is fed by a channel of air that moves in through the door and runs directly to the burning wood in the back. The channel is about two feet wide, and that section is not as hot as the rest of the oven. We use the hearth in front of the oven door (which we had made by the local iron guy) as a place to dry out our kosher salt, which clumps up in the humidity. We toast spices, seeds, and nuts just inside the door. It's easy to keep an eye on them there and monitor the heat.

The pockets directly to the right and the left of the fire in the back are the hottest parts of the oven. This is where we put the food we need to blast with heat. The areas just to the left and the right of the door aren't as hot, but they hold a steady temperature. This part of the oven is heated as much by the thermal mass of the masonry as by the fire in the back. The flames roll down off the ceiling about six inches inside the door. This is where we can finish a dish and crisp up the skin of fish or poultry.

When we cook, we might braise in the area just inside the door, then uncover the pan and crisp up the skin closer to the flame. When it's time to serve the dish, we reheat it and add color by moving it to where the flames loop down just inside the door. We play the oven like it's an instrument, using different parts of it to find the right tone and timbre.

A wood-burning oven isn't just a tool you fire up. A wood-burning oven is alive.

El Almacén

THE LARDER

Suddenly we had a new world of ingredients to discover—the Caribbean was at our fingertips: we could flag down fishermen as they drove their cooler-filled minivans and pickup trucks along the crazy, washed-out road that leads from the port in Punta Allen through the Reserva de la Biósfera Sian Ka'an. Skeptical of us at first, the men opened the coolers to show off seafood that they'd just caught by spear or line: the eyes of the fish still gleaming, the scales reflecting colors we'd never seen before. Even the lobster brought in from the reef seemed otherworldly: all enormous, with meaty tails and no claws.

As we traveled around the region to find affordable building materials, we also became driven in our search for

Preceding: This Yucatán traveler brings us different types of honeys and bee pollen. These natural sweeteners are also good for one's health.

ingredients. Where did the vegetables at the market come from? Then we began to notice Mayas stepping onto the road from little unmarked trails that were at most two feet wide. Soon we were randomly walking into the jungle down these unknown paths. We'd go for miles, and then suddenly, there'd be a small *milpa,* or farm. At first the parched clearings looked like the moon, but gradually we began to see that there were tomatoes, squash, beans, and chiles growing between the rocks, seemingly defying nature to survive under the endless sun.

Drives to distant markets presented us with produce that we had never even seen before. Every day expanded our palates, our Spanish vocabularies, and our dreams for what Hartwood could be.

BUILDING FLAVOR

Our cooking isn't complicated, because our kitchen—humid, smoky, crowded, exposed to the elements—can't pull off anything that calls for extreme precision or control, but the food we produce is complex because we use what's around us to build flavor. Every dish has a balance of sweet and spicy, fresh and dried, oil and acid. So we might cook that fish with habaneros and serve it with a roasted sweet potato basted with dark honey from the state of Tabasco, then finished with some of the chamomile hanging to dry above the grill. We might add charred spring onions rubbed with that roasted chile oil and sprinkled with toasted guajillo chiles that have been pulverized in a spice grinder.

Some of our flavoring elements are very simple: honeys, salts, fresh and dried herbs, fresh and dried chiles. Some take more work. The pickles need time to sit, and the three oils we use—roasted chile oil, roasted garlic oil, and roasted onion oil—take some effort to prepare, but they're essential to this food.

The idea behind the recipes here isn't that far from the mantra you get in so many restaurants—that if you start with the best ingredients, you shouldn't need to do too much to them. But if you take that idea too literally, you might end up doing nothing at all. Instead, the little we do adds layers so that the bright clarity of those fresh ingredients is delivered with fully formed chords of flavors in the background.

You probably won't taste chile in the roasted chile oil. You probably won't even taste the oil. But you will taste something that makes the other elements of the dish snap into focus, and that fish will be unlike any other fish you've grilled. You don't build flavor to overwhelm your senses, you build flavor to heighten the purity of what you're cooking.

Here are some of the ingredients you'll see filling our kitchen crates, lining our pantry shelves, and hanging from the rafters to dry. Our advice on finding the less-familiar ones: almost every town now has a Mexican grocery store. Before you start ordering online, get to know your community.

CHILES

After living in Mexico for a while, you develop a taste for how everybody eats. It's important to get the mix of how to do spicy: tomatoes, pickled onions, vinegar, lime juice, and other ingredients break the heat a little, or bring it out.

Down here, even the dried chiles are a little moister and fresher than the ones you get in the States, which have been sitting for who knows how long (another reason why it's really worth seeking out a Mexican market). Some are sharp and fade quickly, some are long lasting. Some are fruity, some are smoky. Some are faint, some are intense. Sometimes we want a smoky chile with mild heat that fades quickly, other times a fruity chile with mild heat that lingers. It depends on the dish.

Unless otherwise specified, the seeds should be left in. But if you're not used to cooking with chiles, start by using half the seeds and membranes—which is where the heat is—and then work your way up.

ANCHO A dried poblano. Sweet, smoky, kind of raisiny.

ÁRBOL The tiny medium–hot guy is a workhorse at Hartwood. We use the dried chiles in many of our dishes.

CASCABEL A super-flavorful dried round chile with a nutty, smoky aroma. We use it every day in our Roasted Chile Oil (page 63), which it turns a beautiful amber.

CHAWA A dried chile that's sweet and mild, the chawa is close to the Fresno peppers you get in the United States. It has a smooth flavor—a little fruity, with gentle heat that doesn't linger. We rehydrate this chile in water for sauces, or infuse it in a little oil.

CHIPOTLE Another workhorse. A dried jalapeño, the chipotle has a smoky and intense flavor that then drops into the background, which means you can use it for just about anything from fish and shellfish to steak to rabbit.

GUAJILLO The smoky sweetness of this dried chile makes it great with fish and seafood, including shrimp, lobster, and octopus.

HABANERO These super-hot lantern-shaped chiles are typical of the Yucatán. We use them fresh, dried, and powdered. They can be orange, green, or white, depending on ripeness.

HABANERO MANZANA *Manzana* means apple, and the habanero manzana is a larger, fruitier habanero. You have all the fire of a traditional habanero, but the added sugars balance the spiciness somewhat. This is a chile that wants to be roasted.

JALAPEÑO These familiar chiles are easy to find in the states—no matter where you shop, chances are you can get fresh jalapeños. They are especially great pickled; see page 54.

MORITA A close relative of the chipotle, the morita is also a smoked jalapeño. But because it spends less time in the smoker, it is more supple and moist, and a little sweeter. The short smoking time also allows the red color of the vine-ripened chiles to come through.

MORRON *Morron* is the Spanish name for bell pepper. With their natural sugars and high water content, these are perfect for cooking in the wood-burning oven and on the grill.

MULATO A close relation of the poblano, the mulato is allowed to ripen until it's red, and then it's smoked. It has a slightly licoricey, chocolatey flavor. It's one of the building blocks of a classic mole.

ONZA Spicy and slightly sweet, this versatile chile from Oaxaca goes with fish or meat. Onza is not easy to find in Tulum, but when we do, we use it in stews and soups.

PASILLA When you dry the chile chilaca, you get pasilla, which has the dried-fruit flavor of a plum or a raisin. It adds a bass note to salsas and stews, and because it only has a mild heat, you can use it to build flavor without setting fire to your mouth.

PEQUÍN You see this chile growing wild in the jungle. When dried, it's the size of a Tic Tac, and it has a super-sharp heat that explodes on your tongue but disappears almost immediately. It wakes up your palate, then it gets out of the way and lets you taste the rest of the dish.

POBLANO Big, dark, and really subtle, with a slight fruitiness. Poblanos can be cooked down, almost like onions, to give body and flavor to a dish.

SERRANO Great for pork belly. We also thinly slice these to give just a kiss of heat to ceviches.

XCATIC (esh-ka-*teek*) These long, thin chiles look like a banana pepper but are much more spicy. They have a fresh heat that opens up the mouth. These are fantastic pickled. Grill a pork chop, add a pile of minced pickled chiles xcatic with some of the pickle solution, and you have a meal. (See photograph on pages 6 and 7.)

Smoked crickets (bottom, center), or *chapulines*, are always found in our kitchen because they are so addictive. Clockwise from there, you'll see some of our favorite dried chiles, including onza, skinny red árbol, large dark morita, tiny pequín, bright round cascabel, chawa, and smoky chipotle.

FRUIT

Many of the fruits that grow in Mexico also grow in Asia. So if you can't find them at Whole Foods or a Mexican market, check out your local Chinatown.

DRAGON FRUIT This vine-like plant grows pretty much anywhere it wants to: in trees, alongside buildings. The fruit is deep pink with soft thorns; inside, the speckled flesh, dotted with black seeds, looks like the upholstery on an '80s sofa. It's usually used for juice, but the soft, fibrous texture of the fruit is good in salsas or ceviche.

GUANABANA (soursop) The flesh of this tropical fruit combines the creaminess of a banana with a bright, citrusy pineapple-strawberry flavor. It's delicious in juices and ice cream.

MANGO We have eight varieties available to us in the Yucatán, but it's fine to go with the Alphonso mangoes you find at the grocery store.

PLÁTANO MACHO We cook with the *plátano macho,* which is Spanish for "big banana." It's three or four times as big as a conventional banana, and it stands up to intense heat: we roast it in the wood-burning oven. The key is to let it ripen for as long as possible so that it's just on the edge of going bad. You want a taste that's almost fermented, so that the concentrated sweetness of the cooked plátáno isn't cloying. Mexican grocers carry platános machos, as will many specialty markets and even some supermarkets.

PRICKLY PEAR The fruit of certain types of opuntia cactus, this is also called cactus pear or, in Mexico, *tuna roja,* thanks to its vibrant color, which ranges from hot pink to purple when ripe. It has the grainy texture of an overripe pear and the flavor of an extremely mild quince paste.

SARAMUYO (sugar apple or sweetsop) Knobby on the outside, sweet and custardy on the inside.

ZAPOTE NEGRO This large oval fruit has a sticky consistency and caramely flavor that—in our kitchen, at least—make it a natural for sauces. There are many varieties, including mamey, with flavor characteristics that can range from overripe pear to almost-fermented plum.

HOW TO SUPRÊME CITRUS

This is a classic restaurant technique for trimming off all the peel and bitter pith and separating the sections from the membranes so that all that is left is fruit. The secret is to use a super-sharp knife, which will cut with little effort; if the knife is dull, you'll need to apply some pressure, and that's where you get into trouble.

First, slice off the top and bottom of the fruit so that you see two tiny circles of flesh. Then, slice off the skin, pith, and outer membrane, following the curvature of the fruit. Trim off any white patches left after you cut off all the peel.

Now you can either stop here and just cut the fruit into ½-inch slices, or you can follow this standard chef's technique. Holding the fruit in one hand and the knife in the other, working over a small bowl, slice as close as possible to the membranes that separate the sections: Slice along one, then the other, and flick the loosened section into the bowl. When the entire fruit has been sectioned, squeeze the juice from the remaining membranes with your hand and reserve for another use.

DRYING HERBS

There are always herbs drying in our kitchen, usually chamomile (which is called *manzanilla* here and grows abundantly), basil, and avocado leaves (which have a light, anise-like perfume). We tie big bunches of them together with twine at the base of the stems so that the leaves—and, in the case of the chamomile, the flowers—will be exposed to the circulating air. Tulum is humid, but the air above the grill and the wood-burning oven is dry, so the chamomile and basil will be ready in a day, the avocado leaves in a day and a half. We aren't drying the herbs to preserve them; fresh herbs are always in season here. Instead, we dry them to concentrate the flavor and to use as a final finish to a dish: right before the runner picks up a whole grilled fish, for example, it gets a dusting of crumbled dried chamomile. It's doubtful that most diners recognize the taste of the dried chamomile, or avocado leaf, or even basil, but there's a subtle note that registers on some level.

Calabaza is plentiful in the Yucatán. Its white stripes and beautiful green color stand out in the market. Pictured also is chayote on the vine, alongside the enormous avocado: lime-green and delicious.

VEGETABLES

CALABAZA LOCAL This soft-skinned, warm-weather, green Yucatán squash is delicious shaved raw into a salad.

CHAYA We think of *chaya* as Mexican spinach. This extremely nutritious green grows wild, protecting itself with a prickly toxin that disappears when the leaves are cooked or juiced. (When cleaning it, be sure to wear latex gloves.)

CHAYOTE Part of the gourd family, this wrinkly pear-shaped vegetable (it's also called vegetable pear) has the qualities of a firm cucumber combined with a melon. It adds crispness and a refreshing bite to salads.

JICAMA If you're not familiar with jicama, you're in for a treat. The plant is a vine, but you use the bulbous tuber, which is crisp and refreshing and a little sweet: imagine crossing an apple with a potato and a cucumber. It's easy to handle. You trim off the thin skin, then cut the knob into slices or batons. Jicama can be as small as a tangerine or as big as a jumbo grapefruit, but size matters less than firmness: you want it to be taut and heavy. Jicama used to be hard to find, but now you can buy it at most specialty stores and even some supermarkets.

NOPALES With a unique flavor that is sometimes compared to green beans, *nopales* (or cactus paddles or pads) are delicious grilled. They are very high in vitamin C and calcium. When cleaning, be sure to cut away the needles with the grain, not against it, and trim away any rough patches.

YUCA A super-fibrous, starchy root, also called *cassava*. When cooked, it's like a cross between a potato and celery root; we love to mash yuca like potatoes.

HERBS AND SPICES

AVOCADO LEAF The avocado leaf has a distinctive licoricey taste we love. We add whole dried leaves to roasts and soups, and we use crumbled dried leaves as seasoning. Often we'll add a pinch of crumbled dried leaves to give a dish a final dusting of flavor. It's important to use young avocado leaves, like the ones we hang up in the kitchen to dry.

BEE POLLEN All you need is a pinch of bee pollen to give a dish an extra dimension. The flavor is distinctive, and the intense yellow color adds visual impact to any composition. You can find bee pollen at health food stores and at the honey stand at most farmers' markets

CANELA Mexican cinnamon is softer and has a gentler flavor than regular supermarket cinnamon. Of course, you can use what you've got in your kitchen cabinet.

CHAMOMILE Chamomile grows abundantly down here, so we always have bunches of it hanging up to dry. We add it to braises for its delicate floral flavor or to roasts as you would thyme. It also works nicely as a finishing herb, crumbled over fish, meat, vegetables—everything, really.

EPAZOTE An intense flavor that is somewhere between tarragon and anise. We use epazote to add lots of brightness to soups, braises, and beans. If you can't find it, use tarragon or fennel sprigs.

HOJA SANTA Literally "sacred leaf"; also known as Mexican pepper leaf. These large, heart-shaped leaves have a flavor reminiscent of eucalyptus, mint, tarragon, and black pepper. Locals use them to wrap fish, to flavor green moles, and to make a liquor called *verdin*. Also excellent in ceviches, marinades, and stocks.

JAMAICA (hibiscus) We use the dried blossoms for infusions that are mixed into cocktails. There's probably hibiscus tea in your grocery store's tea section (it's great for stomachaches) and you didn't even know it. Definitely try it in cocktails too.

PIMIENTO DE TABASCO If the clove-like sweetness of this dried berry seems familiar, that's because it's allspice—albeit more dusty and peppercorny than what you get in the States.

SAL DE GUSANO This is salt mixed with chile and ground toasted dried worms. Typically used to rim glasses of mezcal, it's also a fantastic (and high-protein!) seasoning for fish. It is available at Mexican groceries.

YERBA BUENA In Mexico, *yerba buena*, which means "good herb," is the name used for a variety of different mints. The one we use has a spearmint-like flavor that is very refreshing.

The aroma of toasting pepitas in a dry, well-seasoned skillet permeates the kitchen each morning. It's hard to keep from eating them all in the course of a day.

SEEDS AND NUTS

Toasted seeds give many of our dishes texture and depth. (They also make a great snack while working on the line.) To toast seeds, heat a dry skillet over medium heat. Add the seeds and cook, tossing occasionally, until they're lightly browned and fragrant. Keep an eye on them—they can burn quickly.

AMARANTH The seeds of the amaranth plant are small, easy to cook, and packed with nutrients. Amaranth is a superfood along the lines of quinoa. We cook the grains into a porridge, and we buy puffed amaranth to use as a garnish. You can find amaranth grains in health food stores and at some specialty markets.

NUEZ DE RAMÓN The fruit of a Maya tree that grows in the interior of the Yucatán. The nuts are pulverized and used in the local masa, giving it its distinct flavor. You can substitute Brazil nuts or even chestnuts.

PEPITAS When you go to a market here, you see *pepitas* (pumpkin seeds) in all stages: fresh in the shell, fresh and shelled, dried in the shell, dried and shelled, and dried, shelled, and ground into powder. Toasted pepitas add an earthy note to a sauce or a dressing—the key is to use just a little so the effect is subtle. They also make a dramatic garnish when crushed. Just like the Maya, we use pepitas nonstop.

SUNFLOWER SEEDS These have a less pronounced flavor than pepitas. We use them as a garnish and as a way to bring a crunchy texture to a dish. We also use the sprouts (see below).

ON SUNFLOWER SPROUTS

If you can't find sunflower sprouts at a health food store or specialty produce market, sprout your own. Simply rinse ½ cup hulled sunflower seeds (or the amount the recipe calls for) very thoroughly in a fine-mesh sieve until the water runs clear. Put the seeds in a large bowl or jar and cover with 1½ cups water (or enough to cover by several inches). Let soak for at least 8 hours, or overnight, until the seeds begin to split and sprouts become visible. Drain in a sieve and rinse again until the water runs clear.

The brooding amber color and subtle floral hints of honey from a milpa, or farm, outside Tulum grace almost every dish and drink at Hartwood.

SWEETENERS

AGAVE This is nectar of some of the same plants from which mezcal is made. Its mellow flavor melds beautifully with the heat of chiles, and it's been one of our favorite kitchen discoveries in Mexico. (We also use fresh agave paddles to cover pork ribs in place of parchment to prevent the meat from drying out in the oven.) Our agave is simply the nectar from the aged leaves of the plant—nothing else is added. We discovered it by accident when trying to find a *pulque* dealer at a market in the interior. When buying it in the United States, select amber grade blue agave, preferably organic.

HONEY Thanks to the incredible variety of exotic fruits and flowers here, Yucatán honey is unlike any other we've tasted. We use rich mamey honey to finish dishes and a lighter "common" honey in braises. (Unlike agave, which blends with the heat of chiles, honey balances it.) Buy the best honey you can find, and keep in mind that the darker the color, the more intense the flavor.

PILONCILLO Until relatively recently, these caramel-colored cones or disks of unrefined sugar were all you could buy here. Although you can now get refined sugar easily, *piloncillo*'s crazy-sweet, round flavor is great for traditional baking.

MEZCAL

In Mexico, they say that this smoky, distilled alcohol is used for everything good—and everything bad. We use it to add instant smokiness to ceviches and sauces. When buying, always look for single-village, preferably organic mezcal. It's important that you can trace the source—that way, you know that it's not hugely manufactured, no chemicals were added, and that the workers were fairly treated. Ours comes from Oaxaca: it's sold in big plastic containers, no name or brand.

LOS PICKLES

These pickle recipes, and the recipes for roasted oils that follow, are at the heart of our food. They line our open shelves and layer so many Mexican flavors into our dishes. The Spanish word for pickles is *encruditos,* but in our kitchen, they're simply called *los pickles.* We use them in almost every dish.

Pickles are what provide the little bursts of flavor that clean your palate, provoke your senses, and prepare you for another bite. It doesn't matter how delicious the grilled fish or perfect the glazed pork belly; without the contrast and arousal you get from, say, a bite of pickled radish or pineapple, you would get bored eating it.

We make most of our pickles with a simple cold brine solution because we're not preserving these ingredients so much as focusing their flavors. Most of the following pickles are best refrigerated for at least 4 hours before using, or overnight, in order to allow the flavors to develop, but you can use them sooner if you must. They will keep in the refrigerator for a week.

Almost all the pickles below work the same way: slice up what you're going to pickle and put it into a jar, mix the brine solution, and pour it in. These recipes are designed to work for a 1-pint Mason jar, but the yield from the produce you use might be different from what we get in the Yucatán. If you have too much solution, don't use it all; if you have too little, give the jar a shake every so often to distribute the liquid. Don't limit yourself to the following recipes—once you get the hang of it, start pickling all your favorite produce.

Pickles, top row, left to right: Spring onions, jalapeños, and habaneros Middle row: Radishes, nance, and red onions Bottom: Pickled jamaica egg

PICKLED WHITE ONIONS

1 white onion, thinly sliced on a mandoline or with a sharp knife

1 cup white vinegar

1 tablespoon sugar

1½ teaspoons kosher salt

PICKLED RED ONIONS

1 red onion, thinly sliced on a mandoline or with a sharp knife

1 cup white vinegar

¼ cup fresh lime juice (from 2 to 3 limes)

¼ cup sugar

1 tablespoon kosher salt

PICKLED RADISHES

2 bunches small radishes (about 24), trimmed and quartered (2 cups)

½ cup white vinegar

½ cup fresh lime juice (from 5 to 6 limes)

1 tablespoon kosher salt

PICKLED JALAPEÑOS

2 cups thinly sliced jalapeños (5 or 6 medium or 10 to 12 small) with seeds intact, stems removed

1 cup white vinegar

2 tablespoons sugar

1½ teaspoons kosher salt

PICKLED NANCE

2 cups nance fruit (left whole)

4 pieces dried chile chawa

1 cup white vinegar

1½ teaspoons kosher salt

PICKLED SPRING ONIONS

8 spring onions, trimmed and halved, bulbs separated and stalks trimmed to 3-inch lengths

3 habaneros (left whole)

1 cup white vinegar

1 tablespoon sugar

1½ teaspoons kosher salt

PICKLED RED BELL PEPPERS

1 large or 2 small red bell peppers, cored, seeded, and cut into long strips	½ cup white vinegar
	2 tablespoons sugar
½ cup water	½ teaspoon kosher salt

PICKLED GREENS

1 bunch beet greens or mustard greens, thoroughly washed and stemmed	1 tablespoon kosher salt
	1 cup white vinegar
2 tablespoons sugar	⅓ cup water

Put the greens in a medium bowl, sprinkle with the sugar and salt, toss, and let wilt for 30 minutes.

Drain the greens and transfer to a 1-pint canning jar. Combine the vinegar and water and pour over the greens, making sure they are completely submerged. Cover and refrigerate for at least 1 hour before using.

PICKLED NOPALES

2 nopales (cactus paddles)	½ teaspoon kosher salt
½ habanero	1 cup white vinegar
2 tablespoons sugar	

Carefully remove the thorns from the nopales by skimming the surface with a chef's knife in the same direction as the thorns. Cut off the woody stems and discard. Cut the cactus into 1-inch cubes, put in a 1-pint canning jar, and add the remaining ingredients. Let sit for at least 4 hours before using. (Note: The pickles and brine will have a rather slimy texture—this is normal with nopales.)

Top row: Pickled spring onions and pickled xcatic
Middle row: Pickled red onions and pickled nance
Bottom row: Pickled radishes

PICKLED HABANEROS WITH CHILE PEQUÍN

2 cups habaneros, left whole

1 tablespoon pequín chiles

1 tablespoon coriander seeds, toasted in a small dry skillet until fragrant

1 cup white vinegar

½ cup sugar

1 tablespoon kosher salt

Let sit, refrigerated, for 2 days before serving.

PICKLED CHAYOTE

½ dried ancho chile, ripped into 2 or 3 pieces

2 dried árbol chiles

1 dried pequín chile

1 cup white vinegar

2 tablespoons sugar

1 tablespoon kosher salt

1½ chayotes, peeled, seeds removed, and sliced

Toast the chiles in a dry cast-iron skillet over medium-low heat until fragrant, about 2 minutes.

Mix together the vinegar, sugar, and salt. Put the chayote slices in a 1-pint canning jar and add the toasted peppers and pickle solution. Let sit for at least 3 hours before using.

YUCATÁN PICKLE PLATE
One of our bar snacks is a plate of whatever pickles look most beautiful that day. It's a good foil for mezcals, or something for a table to share as a palate cleanser just before the main courses arrive. At home, a pickle plate is also a great way to serve those that you have in the fridge. Just be sure that you include some pickled jamaica eggs, which will anchor the composition and give it heft. Clockwise from top: Pickled nance; pickled piña; pickled sandia; spring onion with pickled habanero; pickled chayote; pickled nopales; pickled radishes. Center: pickled jamaica egg.

PICKLED SANDIA

3 cups water

1 tablespoon plus 1 teaspoon
    kosher salt

2 cups 1-inch squares peeled
    watermelon rind
    (a little red is okay)

1 cup white vinegar

¼ cup sugar

Bring water to boil in a medium saucepan and add 1 tablespoon of the salt. Add the watermelon rind, cover, reduce the heat so that the water is at a low boil, and cook for about 30 minutes, until the watermelon rind is soft. Drain the rind and let cool.

Combine the vinegar, sugar, and the remaining 1 teaspoon salt. Put the rind in a 1-pint canning jar and add the pickle solution. Let sit for at least 3 hours before using.

PICKLED PIÑA

⅓ ripe pineapple, peeled, cored,
    and cut into
    ¾-inch-thick rounds

2 tablespoons olive oil

¼ cup honey

Pinch of kosher salt,
    plus 1 teaspoon

1 dried árbol chile

½ cinnamon stick

1 teaspoon allspice berries

½ teaspoon black peppercorns

1 cup apple cider vinegar

2 tablespoons sugar

Prepare a hot fire in a grill. Toss the pineapple with the olive oil and honey in a medium bowl and season with a generous pinch of salt. Grill over high heat, turning once, until marked by the grill and cooked through, about 1 minute per side. Let cool, then cut into wedges. Set aside.

Toast the chile, cinnamon, allspice, and peppercorns in a dry cast-iron skillet over medium heat until fragrant, about 2 minutes. Set aside.

Heat the vinegar, sugar, and the remaining 1 teaspoon salt in a small saucepan over medium-low heat, stirring, until the sugar and salt dissolve. Put the pineapple in a 1-pint canning jar and add the toasted chiles and spices. Add the pickle solution. Let sit for at least 3 hours before using.

PICKLED JAMAICA EGGS

MAKES 12 PICKLED EGGS

12 large eggs

4 cups white vinegar

1 cup dried jamaica
(hibiscus) flowers

1 cup sugar

1 tablespoon kosher salt

Fill a large saucepan with water and bring to a rolling boil. Add the eggs, carefully lowering them into the water with a spider or a slotted spoon, and cook for exactly 8 minutes. While the eggs are cooking, fill a large bowl with ice and water.

Remove the eggs from the boiling water with the spider or slotted spoon and put into the ice bath. When the eggs are cool enough to handle, remove and carefully peel. Put the peeled eggs in a large jar or other nonreactive container.

Mix together the vinegar, jamaica flowers, sugar, and salt. Add the pickle solution to the eggs and let sit for at least 2 hours, stirring the eggs every 20 minutes, so that the solution makes its way to all of the surfaces (if not, the eggs will remain white where they are touching and look polka-dotted—which isn't the worst thing). The color will intensify the longer the eggs pickle, and the jamaica flowers will make the solution (and eggs) more tart; taste until you decide it's time to drain them. The drained eggs will keep for 3 days covered in the refrigerator.

Clockwise from top: Pickled nopales, piña, and jamaica egg

ROASTED OILS

These oils are the workhorses of the kitchen. The process is simple: we pour oil into a roasting pan (at home you can use a deep sturdy pan), add chiles, garlic, or onions, and roast until the oil is flavored, then let cool.

Chiles, garlic, and onions might seem too pungent, but these oils are actually quite subtle. Most important, these oils create flavor in every dish they touch. We use them as both cooking and finishing oils for pretty much everything we serve. We'll use an oil to season a piece of meat before it goes on the grill, then drizzle on a little more just before we send out the dish. Even something as simple as pouring a splash of one of these oils into a cast-iron pan before you sauté vegetables will add another dimension you might not quite be able to place but that will transform the dish.

We make the oils in 5-liter batches, and we work through them quickly. The recipes here are for 1-liter batches, which might seem like a lot, but they're easy to make, and the payoff is tremendous. If refrigerated, they will keep for up to 2 weeks. Each recipe is designed to be made in a 10-inch pan. If you use a cast-iron skillet, use a deep one, and handle with some caution. First, don't overfill it: there should be ample space between the oil and the top of the pan. Second, proceed carefully: take it very slowly when you lift the pan out of the oven. (If you prefer, you can use a 12-inch pan or a 10-inch Dutch oven.)

At Hartwood, we don't use pure olive oil, because it breaks down more quickly when exposed to heat. Good-quality olive oil has a low smoke point, and almost everything you like about it will disappear after some time in the oven. Instead, we use a blend of canola and olive oils, which is what most restaurants do. At home, you can use a blended oil or a basic, inexpensive olive oil—save the good stuff for your salads.

Ideally, you'll make all three of these oils and incorporate them into your cooking, but the fact is, you don't have to make them in order to cook from this book: you can just substitute regular olive oil. Still, we encourage you to make at least one. Start with the roasted garlic oil: you're not only infusing the oil, you're also making garlic confit, and those soft, flavorful cloves are another foundation of many of our dishes.

ROASTED GARLIC OIL AND ROASTED GARLIC

MAKES ABOUT 1 LITER (ABOUT 4 CUPS) OIL, PLUS ROASTED GARLIC

This recipe gives you two foundations of flavor. The oil, which tastes sweet and buttery, is one of the key elements in our grilled octopus (page 137). But the roasted garlic is integral to so much of what we cook that we would make the oil just to get the cloves. We use the oil in dressings and sauces and to flavor the leafy greens we serve with meat dishes.

6 whole heads garlic	3 oregano sprigs
3 thyme sprigs	One 1-liter bottle olive oil

Preheat the oven to 350°F.

Slice off the top ½ inch of each garlic head so that most of the cloves are exposed. Put the garlic in a deep sturdy 10-inch pan with the herbs and add enough olive oil so that the heads are just above the surface. Cover with parchment paper, then tightly cover the pan with foil. Roast for 45 minutes, or until the garlic is soft—check by piercing a head with a paring knife. Remove the parchment and foil and roast for 5 more minutes to brown the garlic a bit. Let cool.

Strain the oil into a 1-liter measuring cup; set the garlic aside. Return the oil to its original bottle (simply pour though a funnel set into the neck of the bottle). Cover the oil and keep in a cool, dark place (the oil will last longer if you refrigerate it; just be sure to take it out about an hour before cooking to liquefy).

Put the garlic heads in a bowl to collect the oil. Then separate the cloves and squeeze the pulp into a pint jar. Discard the papery skin and herbs. Strain the oil that collected in the bowl and use to cover the garlic; add more of the garlic oil if necessary to cover it. Cover and refrigerate; the roasted garlic will keep for up to 2 weeks.

ROASTED CHILE OIL

MAKES ABOUT 1 LITER (ABOUT 4 CUPS)

We use mild cascabel chiles for our chile oil, which give it a pleasantly toasty, smoky flavor. Cascabel chiles are easy to find in the Yucatán. We buy them by the shopping bag. In the United States, look for them in a Mexican market or online.

24 dried cascabel chiles (about 4 ounces)

1 red onion, quartered

3 thyme sprigs

3 oregano sprigs

3 bay leaves

One 1-liter bottle olive oil

Preheat the oven to 350°F.

Combine the chiles, onion, and herbs in a deep sturdy 10-inch pan. Pour in enough olive oil to cover. Cover the pan with foil and roast for 1½ hours. Let cool.

Strain the oil into a 1-liter measuring cup; discard the solids. Return the oil to its original bottle (simply pour through a funnel set into the neck of the bottle). Cover and keep in a cool, dry place (it will last longer in the fridge; just be sure to take it out about an hour before cooking to liquefy).

ROASTED ONION OIL AND BURNT ONIONS

MAKES ABOUT 1 LITER (ABOUT 4 CUPS) OIL, PLUS BURNT ONIONS

You want to crowd the pan with the onions so that exposed tops will unfurl and blacken in the oven. We use the onions in our Grilled Calamar Salad (page 140) and other dishes, and you can always find some under our whole grilled fish. At home, you would probably not roast a pan full of onions just to use a few to round out a dish, but if you keep some in a jar in the refrigerator, you'll have a shortcut to the kind of complexity you find on a restaurant menu—plus the onion oil. We drizzle the oil over grilled steaks, octopus, and vegetables.

8 medium or 10 small white onions, quartered

One 1-liter bottle olive oil

½ teaspoon kosher salt

Freshly ground black pepper to taste

Preheat the oven to 450°F.

Put the onions in a deep sturdy 10-inch pan and add enough olive oil so that just about ½ inch of the tops of the onions is exposed. Season with the salt and pepper. Roast for 45 minutes, or until the tops of the onions are black; if necessary, turn on the broiler for the last 5 minutes to char the onions. Let cool.

Strain the oil into a 1-liter measuring cup; reserve the onions. Return the oil to its original bottle (simply pour through a funnel set into the neck of the bottle). Cover the oil and keep in a cool, dry place (it will last longer in the fridge; just take it out about an hour before cooking to liquefy). Keep the onions covered and refrigerated.

THE CAST-IRON ARSENAL

We swear by cast iron. We have a stack of skillets that we use both in the oven and on the grill, because nothing holds temperature like cast iron, and because it can take the heat—the pans won't bow or warp or shatter. If we lost our cast-iron pans, it's hard to say what we would do.

Our arsenal took years to accumulate. At first we had twelve 10-inch skillets and a couple of smaller ones that we used for sides. We brought them down in our luggage, paying the overweight fee. Then we brought down 13-inch skillets, and more smaller skillets for sauces.

You need to care for cast iron with love. We don't wash our pans with soap and water. Instead, we scour them with a metal scrubber and then oil them so they are ready to use again. At the end of the night, all the pans are wiped clean, oiled, and stacked with paper towels between them—the paper absorbs the oil, which helps to distribute it all over the cooking surface during the night. And if a rain blows in, the paper will help with oxidation, though the edges of the pans might be dotted with rust.

If you don't have a cast-iron pan, now's the time to get one. The one essential piece of cast iron you should have is a 10-inch skillet. When you buy it, you need to season it. Everybody has their own technique; ours is described below.

SEASON YOUR PAN

1. Heat the oven to 225°F. Scrub the pan with soap and water (this is the only time soap and water will touch it) and dry carefully.

2. Use a paper towel to coat the entire pan with a thin film of canola oil. Pour in 1 tablespoon kosher salt and rub the pan with the paper towel to lightly scour the surface. Wipe out the salt (it's fine if you don't get all of it) and put the pan in the oven for 2 hours, flipping the pan over once halfway through.

3. Let the pan cool completely, then repeat step 2, increasing the oven temperature to 350°F.

CENOTE WORLD

Once you've gotten your fill of the Caribbean Sea in Tulum—
which might never happen—you graduate to what we call
Cenote World. There are some six thousand *cenotes*, or
fresh water caves, hidden throughout the Yucatán. They
have a magical connotation in Maya mythology, which
considers them the underworld. They also have real powers
for farmers, as the roots of their plants grow down deep to
seek the crystal-clear water. The openings can be body-
size holes covered with vines, or craters the size of a house.
Some cenotes are full-on tourist attractions, complete with
billboards and snack bars; others just have a handwritten
cardboard sign and a guy in a beach chair taking pesos. The
best ones are local secrets.

It can be unnerving to look into one of these black holes
in the ground: it's like staring into the abyss—or the Garden
of Eden, depending on your mind-set—but once you climb
down and dive in, the cold water is so pure and refreshing and
the solitude so complete, you forget about the stalactites
and bats. In summer, when it's 95°F and humid, we'll run
to one that's less than half a mile away to cool off. Our
bartender, Rob, is a dive guide who has explored the cenotes
extensively—he knows the hidden channels, the openings
you can't get to on foot. He goes exploring with a group who
have found everything from skulls and altars to Maya gold
and pieces of woolly mammoth bone. Not all the cenotes have
been documented. Divers first started coming down in the
1980s, and they're still mapping the underground system.

El Mercado

<u>THE MARKET</u>

Everything is in constant motion at the markets in the Yucatán, the activity stretching from the morning into the afternoon. It's like being transported to another world. This is where you gain the knowledge you put to use in the kitchen, and the best ideas start with a simple conversation with the vendors. What's the name of this? How is it used? What is it similar to?

It's humbling to ask such basic questions and to sound like you have

Preceding: We buy *miel de mamey* from this Maya woman, who joked that our honey was nothing compared to what she had to sell, and she was right. It's a rare honey that bees make from the pollen of mamey flowers.

no idea what you're doing, but that's how you learn. This area has so many ingredients that are barely documented in Spanish, never mind in English, that you need to start at the beginning. Once you get over your pride, you start to draw in information like a dry sponge sucks up water. Sometimes you are exposed to so much it can feel like a chemical rush. You can get addicted to the markets—addicted to new ingredients, addicted to discovery, addicted to learning.

When we inspected the plot where we would build the restaurant, we found a twenty-foot-long jicama vine growing wild. It was insane. The vine was so large it was taking over entire trees.

Jicama is starchy and crisp and completely refreshing. Imagine crossing a potato, an apple, and a cucumber without the seeds. Jicama is almost entirely water by weight, so when you shop for it, look for the firmest and heaviest. You want the skin to be tight, not wrinkled.   SERVES 6

JICAMA SALAD with MINT CREMA

2 jicamas (each about the size of a small grapefruit)

2 oranges, suprêmed (see page 45)

1 cup mint leaves

1 teaspoon kosher salt

½ cup Lime and Honey Vinaigrette (page 82)

¾ cup Mint Crema

3 tablespoons Prickly Pear Preserves (recipe follows; optional)

½ cup pepitas (pumpkin seeds), toasted in a dry skillet until lightly browned

½ cup sunflower seeds, toasted in a dry skillet until lightly browned

Peel the jicama with a vegetable peeler or sharp paring knife and cut into ¼-inch-thick slices, about 2 inches by 1½ inches. Put in a bowl and add the orange suprêmes, mint, and salt, then add the vinaigrette and toss to coat.

Coat the bottom of each serving dish with a smear of the mint crema and pile the salad on top. Drizzle with the prickly pear preserves, if using, and sprinkle the pepitas and sunflower seeds over the top.

MINT CREMA

MAKES ABOUT 1½ CUPS

8 pepitas (pumpkin seeds), toasted in a dry skillet until lightly browned

1 cup mint leaves

½ cup olive oil

1 tablespoon honey

½ teaspoon fresh lime juice

½ cup water

⅓ cup sour cream

1 teaspoon kosher salt, or to taste

Combine the pepitas, mint, olive oil, honey, and lime juice in a blender and blend on high speed until smooth and emulsified. Slowly add the water and blend until emulsified, about 30 seconds, then add the sour cream and salt and blend for another 10 seconds. The crema should be as thick as aioli. Season to taste if necessary. Transfer to a bowl, cover, and refrigerate until ready to use.

We garnish this salad with
Prickly Pear Preserves, but
you could use a handful
of ripe watermelon cubes
instead. And, yes, the
mint crema recipe makes
double what you'll need,
but we promise you'll want
to make this salad again.

PRICKLY PEAR PRESERVES

MAKES ABOUT ¼ CUP

In order to preserve the beautiful dark–purple color of the prickly pears, be sure to cook the preserves over medium heat so they simmer, not boil. Keep an eye on them toward the end of cooking; overcooking can also turn them brown.

2 prickly pears

One ½–inch piece ginger, peeled and cut into ¼–inch slices

1 tablespoon white vinegar

1 tablespoon water

1 tablespoon sugar

¼ teaspoon kosher salt

Remove the skin from the prickly pears. Put the flesh in a bowl and break it apart with a spoon until liquefied.

Combine the prickly pear, ginger, vinegar, water, sugar, and salt in a medium-size saucepan, bring to a simmer over medium heat and simmer until the liquid is reduced by half and syrupy, 20 to 25 minutes. Let cool, then strain out the seeds and ginger.

ON THE ROAD

We shop at the markets in Tulum, but almost everything sold here comes from one of the larger regional marketplaces. The closest is in Valladolid, which is about two hours away and handles all the produce grown in the area.

Another thirty minutes north, and you're in Tizimín, which is known for papaya, *makal* (a tuber with a distinctively nutty flavor), and different kinds of yuca. There you can find *dulce de calabaza*, pictured on page 217, made by punching holes in the squash with a screwdriver, then submerging it in honey for about five days, until the skin is soft. The flesh is sweet and dark, and the flavor is slightly fermented and almost molasses-like. You can make it yourself, but it's easier to buy it.

Merida, two hours west of Valladolid, doesn't have any produce you can't find in Valladolid or Tizimín, but it has the best restaurant supplies in the area. This is where we pick up plates, glasses, and ox-handled knives for the restaurant. And Merida is the only place that sells hand-cranked juicers that can stand up to high use in the humid and salty air. We went through dozens of manual juicers before somebody on staff thought to buy one of these.

The largest wholesale marketplace in the region is in the small town of Oxkutzcab, a three-and-a-half hour drive from Tulum. The market is a big box of a building in the middle of town—there's nothing precious about it. There are no tourists, nothing to do but buy goods in bulk. Most of the produce is sold in the square outside the building, and the transactions are straightforward: the price is the price, and the price is the same no matter which vendor you go to. This market supplies many of the other markets in the area—what you find in Oxkutzcab, you'll see in Tulum in a day or two.

A trip to any of these markets will take most of the day. You drive there, stop for a lunch of *pollo asado* with lime and chile, with tortillas and rice on the side, then shop and drive back. Sometimes you might get stopped at a roadblock operated by the Federales, the national police force: they wear black body armor, obscure their faces with ski masks, carry automatic

weapons, and work in large numbers. There's always one of them standing next to a high-caliber machine gun mounted to the back of a pickup, the ammunition belt locked and loaded. Message received. Although you never have any trouble with them, it takes a little while for them to go through your paperwork, and for you to explain why an American is driving to the coast with a carload of fresh fruit.

In other words, it doesn't make much practical sense to go to the markets: you do it because you want to learn.

Just as important, you do it because the hours you spend on the road might be the only time you get to yourself. Driving through the jungle is therapy. You get in your truck, head out early, and let the clutter that fills your mind fall away. You don't play music or catch up on phone calls. You just drive, because that's when you can allow yourself to stop worrying about the details and start to think. When you're working in a busy restaurant and all the tables are full, you need to be able to ignore the chaos and do your job. This kind of work tends to attract a particular kind of person, which is maybe why a lot of chefs are drawn to the kitchen: you build mental focus to isolate yourself in that crowded room. But it's not the same as being alone. How do you know who you are, and what you can do without facing yourself in silence? How do you know what you can create? There needs to be a place you can go to inside your mind. The seven-hour drive to Oxkutzcab and back is a block of time that you can spend in self-examination. Sometimes you need to be introverted.

Walking down this road many times,
we've often wanted to stop, set up a
hammock in the trees, and take in the air
and the sounds of the woods.

This salad plays the fresh flavors of papaya and grapefruit against the earthiness of the lentils. It's bright and fruity, but it's also substantial. The chunks of papaya and grapefruit in the salad are echoed by a papaya and grapefruit sauce you make in the blender (you'll have extra—drink it straight while you cook), and the whole dish comes together with a lime and honey vinaigrette you'll want to use for pretty much every other salad you make. Amaranth greens are increasingly easy to find at farmers' markets in the summer.   SERVES 6

LENTIL and PAPAYA SALAD with LIME and HONEY VINAIGRETTE

1 cup dried lentils (French, brown, or red)

2 cups water

Kosher salt

1 white onion, halved

1 carrot, peeled and halved

3 bay leaves

Freshly ground black pepper

½ cup Lime and Honey Vinaigrette (recipe follows), or as needed

½ bunch amaranth, leaves only (or kale or chard, torn into 1-inch pieces)

2 grapefruit, suprêmed (see page 45)

1 summer squash, thinly sliced

½ papaya, peeled, seeded, and cut into 1-inch pieces

½ lime (optional)

1 cup Papaya Grapefruit Sauce (recipe follows)

Puffed amaranth seeds for garnish (optional)

Cook the lentils: Combine the lentils, water, 2 teaspoons salt, the onion, carrot, and bay leaves in a large saucepan. Bring to a rolling boil over medium heat and cook for 15 minutes. Check to see if the lentils are tender; depending on the type of lentils, it may take up to another 15 minutes to cook them. Remove from the heat, drain, and cool, then discard the onion, carrot, and bay leaves and season lentils with salt and pepper.

Put the lentils in a medium bowl and toss with the vinaigrette. Taste and adjust the seasoning as necessary. Add the amaranth leaves and toss. Add the grapefruit suprêmes, squash, and papaya and toss gently—the fruit will break apart some, but you don't want the pieces to turn to mush. Taste and adjust the seasoning, adding more vinaigrette if necessary. (Sometimes an extra squeeze of lime is nice too.)

To serve, dab the papaya grapefruit sauce onto six salad plates (or onto a serving platter) and use the back of a spoon to spread it into a swirl. Gently arrange the lentil salad on top and sprinkle with puffed amaranth seeds, if using.

We use both amaranth seeds and the leaves in this recipe. Many people talk about nose-to-tail cooking; we do that not only with fish but with vegetables, plants, and herbs. Using the entire ingredient is a must whenever you get the chance.

LIME AND HONEY VINAIGRETTE

MAKES ABOUT 1 CUP

There are so many limes in Mexico. It's an ingredient that you use for everything: drinks, soups, meat, desserts. So this vinaigrette has lots of applications. You can use it as a marinade, as a way to get proteins started before you put them on the grill or in the oven, or as a finishing touch. It breaks through that smoke and char. And, of course, it's great on salads.

¼ cup fresh lime juice (from 2 to 3 limes), or to taste

¾ cup olive oil

2 tablespoons honey, or to taste

1 teaspoon kosher salt, or to taste

Whisk all the ingredients in a small bowl until emulsified, then taste—everything should be in balance: the acid of the lime, the sweetness of the honey, the salinity of the salt. If anything is too faint, add more of whatever is missing. The vinaigrette will keep for up to a week in the refrigerator; whisk again before serving to re-emulsify it.

PAPAYA GRAPEFRUIT SAUCE

MAKES ABOUT 2 CUPS

½ papaya, peeled, seeded, and cut into 1-inch pieces

½ cup fresh grapefruit juice

¼ cup honey

¼ cup water

1 teaspoon kosher salt

Add all the ingredients to a blender and puree until smooth, about 30 seconds. The sauce should have the consistency of sour cream. It tends to thicken as it stands; if it seems a little too thick, give it a stir to loosen it up.

The tomatoes that grow in the Yucatán are survivalists. These aren't the lush, leafy plants you see in the United States or Italy. They are tough vines with roots that grow down through gaps in the limestone rocks to seek the water veins that feed the cenotes. Sometimes the roots are as long as twenty-five feet. The tomatoes we use come through the market at Valladolid. While parts of Valladolid are a postcard-perfect colonial town, it was built on an ancient Maya city that drew water from the cenotes found within the city limits.

We top the salad with sunflower sprouts from an organic farmer named Christian Klamroth Bermudez. He was one of our first friends down here; we opened the restaurant at about the same time that he started farming in his greenhouses near Coba, a town to the west of Tulum. He now grows every kind of sprout—from lentil to buckwheat to melon. Look for sunflower sprouts in the produce section of a good market or at a health food store. Or sprout your own, a practice that will benefit more than just this dish (see page 49).

SERVES 6

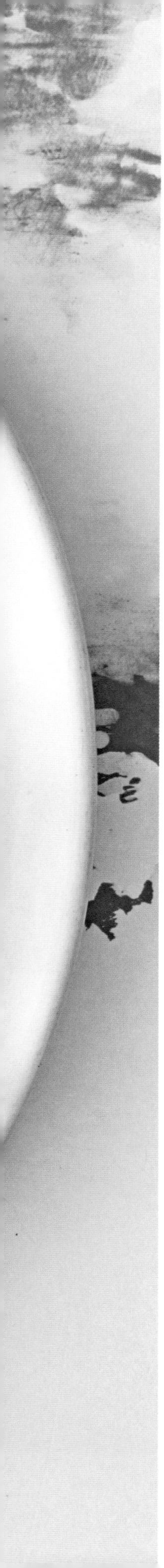

VALLADOLID TOMATO SALAD

DRESSING

1 tablespoon sunflower seeds, toasted in a dry skillet until lightly browned

½ cup basil leaves

1 tablespoon fresh lime juice

¼ teaspoon honey

¼ teaspoon kosher salt

⅓ cup olive oil

6 heirloom tomatoes, cut into 6 wedges each

2 cups sunflower sprouts (see page 49; use 2 cups sunflower seeds for sprouting)

½ cup Pickled Red Onions (page 54)

1 teaspoon kosher salt

¼ cup crumbled queso cotija (or queso fresco, feta, or ricotta salata)

Make the dressing: Combine the sunflower seeds, basil, lime juice, honey, salt, and olive oil in a blender and blend until smooth.

Put the tomatoes in a mixing bowl, add 1½ cups of the sunflower sprouts, the pickled red onions, dressing, and salt, and toss to combine. Arrange on a serving dish and garnish with the cotija and remaining ½ cup sunflower sprouts.

One serving of the Valladolid Tomato Salad, made using heirloom and cherry tomatoes we had on hand at Hartwood that day.

Grilling nopales for the
Grilled Nopales Salad
with Queso Cotija

Nopales, or cactus paddles, are a classic Mexican ingredient that intimidates most Americans—which completely makes sense: they are covered in thorns, and they can be slimy when cooked. The thorns are easy to handle: run the blade of a sharp knife across the surface of the paddle in the direction of the spikes, which are angled like a porcupine's quills. Then you marinate it overnight to get rid of any slime ("la vava"), and throw away everything that seeps out. For this salad, we grill the paddles to get a slight char that offsets the tangy bite of the nopales before marinating them.

It's increasingly easy to find nopales in the United States—lots of better supermarkets now carry them. This recipe also calls for *queso cotija*, a cow's-milk cheese that's salty and crumbly like feta or ricotta salata.

SERVES 2

GRILLED NOPALES SALAD with QUESO COTIJA

1 pound nopales (cactus paddles), spines removed and edges trimmed

1 red bell pepper

1 yellow bell pepper

1 red onion, cut in half

½ cup olive oil, plus more for coating the vegetables

Kosher salt and freshly ground black pepper

2 tablespoons fresh lime juice

½ cup sunflower sprouts (see page 49)

Large pinch of Pickled Red Onions (page 54)

1 ounce queso cotija (or queso fresco, feta, or ricotta salata), crumbled (2 tablespoons)

1 Pickled Jamaica Egg, halved (page 59)

Grated lime zest for garnish

Prepare a grill for high heat.

Put the nopales, peppers, and onion in a large bowl and toss with a bit of olive oil to coat. Season with salt and pepper. Grill the nopales until soft, with good grill marks, about 1 minute per side. Grill the onion until lightly charred, about 4 minutes per side. Grill the peppers, turning occasionally, until the skin is blackened all over. Transfer the vegetables to a cutting board as they are done.

Remove the skin and seeds from the peppers and cut them lengthwise into thin strips. Thinly slice the nopales and onion. Transfer all the vegetables to a bowl, add ¼ cup of the olive oil and the lime juice, and stir to coat. Add salt and pepper to taste. Cover and refrigerate overnight.

When you're ready to serve, drain the vegetables and discard the liquid. Combine the vegetables, sunflower sprouts, pickled red onion, queso cotija, and the remaining ¼ cup olive oil in a bowl and toss to combine. Season with salt and pepper to taste. Garnish with the pickled egg and sprinkle with lime zest and black pepper.

Our take on the traditional Mexican soup is cool and refreshing, with the creamy consistency of a velvety vichyssoise. You first make a light vegetable stock, then puree it with avocados and top the soup with a spicy cabbage and epazote salad. It takes a bit of work, but the soup is substantial enough to serve as a meal on a hot day. When shopping for avocados, look for ones that yield to the touch but not too much: don't buy them when they feel mushy. Epazote may be difficult to find outside Mexican markets, but you can substitute tarragon or fennel fronds.   SERVES 6

CHILLED AVOCADO SOUP with EPAZOTE

VEGETABLE STOCK

1 small white onion, roughly chopped

2 carrots, peeled and roughly chopped

2 celery stalks, roughly chopped

1 teaspoon black peppercorns

½ teaspoon coriander seeds

4 epazote stems (or tarragon stems or fennel fronds)

4 cups water

SOUP

4 large ripe Hass avocados, halved, peeled, and pitted, plus extra slices for garnish

¼ cup fresh lime juice (from 2 to 3 limes)

1½ teaspoons kosher salt, or to taste

3 cups Vegetable Stock (above), or as needed

SALAD

2 cups thinly sliced red cabbage

½ habanero, seeded and minced, or to taste

¼ cup fresh epazote leaves (or tarragon leaves or fennel fronds)

¼ cup small cubes seeded cucumber

¼ cup minced red onion

¼ cup julienned radishes

2 tablespoons Lime and Honey Vinaigrette (page 82)

Make the vegetable stock: Combine the onion, carrots, celery, peppercorns, coriander seeds, epazote stems, and water in a large saucepan. Bring to a simmer and cook for 30 minutes. Let cool.

Strain the stock and refrigerate until chilled.

Make the soup: Combine the avocados, lime juice, salt, and vegetable stock in a blender and blend on high speed until creamy, slowly adding more stock if necessary, until the mixture is the consistency of a cream soup. Taste and add more salt if needed. Transfer to a bowl and refrigerate until just chilled. (You want to serve the soup quickly so it maintains its color.)

Meanwhile, make the salad: Combine the cabbage, habanero, epazote leaves, cucumber, red onion, and radishes in a bowl and toss well. (If you want it spicier, use the whole habanero; if you want it really spicy, keep the seeds in.) Add the vinaigrette and toss again.

To serve, ladle the soup into bowls and place a large spoonful of salad on top of each bowl. Garnish with avocado slices.

CALL JUAN

Juan Couoh Martinez isn't on our payroll, but he might as well be. He's a taxi driver, and he runs errands, delivers ice, and takes staff home at the end of the day. Some of what he does is scheduled, but a lot of it happens because we're short on an ingredient, or a supplier is running late, or somebody forgot to pick up something. The restaurant is only a couple of miles from town, but the beach road is narrow and can be busy in the morning (when the sanitation and water trucks make their stops), and during the day (when the hotels and restaurants get deliveries), and at night (when everybody is going out). It makes more sense to call Juan, who knows all the markets, understands exactly what we want, and is as picky as we are about the level of quality that we demand.

We'll call Juan five, ten, twenty times in a day. The butcher just finished making chorizo according to our recipe? Call Juan. Time to buy more marine-grade varnish to touch up the tables, benches, and posts in the dining area? Call Juan. There's a fresh shipment of coconuts and mangoes at the markets in town? Call Juan. Need to return the packing crates we borrowed to get all those mangoes to the restaurant? Call Juan. "Call Juan" is one of the most common phrases you'll hear in the kitchen.

Juan isn't the only taxi driver who works with the restaurant. Tulum is crawling with taxis, which are painted white with bright red trim and don't charge much. We have a network of drivers on speed dial. (If you visit Tulum, it's easier to get around by taxi than it is dealing with a rental car—parking is a hassle, and the road that runs along the beach works like a single lane that happens to run in two directions.) But we work with Juan every day. When we set out family meal, he'll grab a plate and eat with us, because he's family.

Watermelon is unusual in that it can carry any flavor without losing its identity. Smoke, spice, heat—watermelon will amplify all of that while still tasting like watermelon. And a soup that requires no cooking is a plus at Hartwood. SERVES 4

CHILLED SANDIA SOUP

SOUP

4 cups cubed seedless watermelon

½ habanero, seeded

2 medium red tomatoes, cut into chunks

1 small red onion

1 celery stalk

⅓ cup epazote leaves (optional)

About 1 cup fresh lime juice (from 10 to 12 limes)

Kosher salt

SALAD

2 cups cubed seedless watermelon

½ cup small mango cubes

⅓ cup celery leaves

⅓ cup cilantro leaves

Suprêmes from ½ grapefruit (see page 45)

Juice of ½ lime

Kosher salt and freshly ground black pepper

Amaranth leaves for garnish (optional)

Make the soup: Combine the watermelon, habanero, tomatoes, red onion, celery, epazote, if using, and ½ cup lime juice in a blender and blend on high for 45 to 60 seconds, until well blended. Strain through a colander, not a fine-mesh sieve as you want to keep some of the pulp, but not all of it. (If you want a chunkier soup, feel free to add back a little bit of pulp to your liking.) Add salt and more lime juice to taste. Refrigerate until cold, at least 45 minutes.

Make the salad: Combine the watermelon, mango, celery and cilantro leaves, grapefruit, and lime juice in a bowl and mix well. Season to taste with salt and pepper.

To serve, divide the soup among four serving bowls. Place the salad in the center of the soup. Garnish with amaranth leaves, if using, and black pepper.

Sweet vegetables with a really deep roast are a delicious accompaniment to grilled fish. This dish is a take on a Maya treat of charred sweet potatoes topped with honey. Here a sprinkle of ground toasted pumpkin seeds adds a contrasting crunch, while the dried chamomile brings floral and herbal notes. If you don't have fresh chamomile that you can dry yourself (see page 46), or can't find dried chamomile at your farmers' market, substitute chamomile tea, which is simply the dried flowers; just be sure to buy organic.   SERVES 4

ROASTED CAMOTES with CHAMOMILE, HONEY, and PEPITAS

1 bunch dried chamomile (or the contents of 8 to 10 organic chamomile tea bags)

4 medium sweet potatoes, scrubbed

4 tablespoons unsalted butter, cut into pieces

½ cup honey

¼ cup pepitas (pumpkin seeds), toasted in a dry skillet until lightly browned, then coarsely ground

Preheat the oven to 375°F.

Spread the chamomile in a baking dish, saving a few sprigs for garnish if using dried chamomile (if using tea bags, save the contents of 2 bags for garnish). Put the sweet potatoes on top and fill the dish one-third full with water. Cover with aluminum foil and bake for about 1 hour.

Carefully pull back the foil and check a potato; if it is not soft and cooked all the way through, bake for another 15 minutes or so. Remove from the oven and increase the oven temperature to 400°F. Put a large cast-iron skillet in the oven.

Cut the sweet potatoes in half lengthwise. Add them to the hot skillet, taking care not to burn yourself, then add the butter. Drizzle the sweet potatoes with the honey and roast for about 5 minutes. Baste the potatoes with the melted butter and honey and roast for 8 to 10 minutes longer, until they are nice and crispy around the edges. Take them out of the oven and baste one last time.

Transfer sweet potatoes to plates. Crumble the reserved chamomile leaves over the sweet potatoes, dust them with the ground pepitas, and serve.

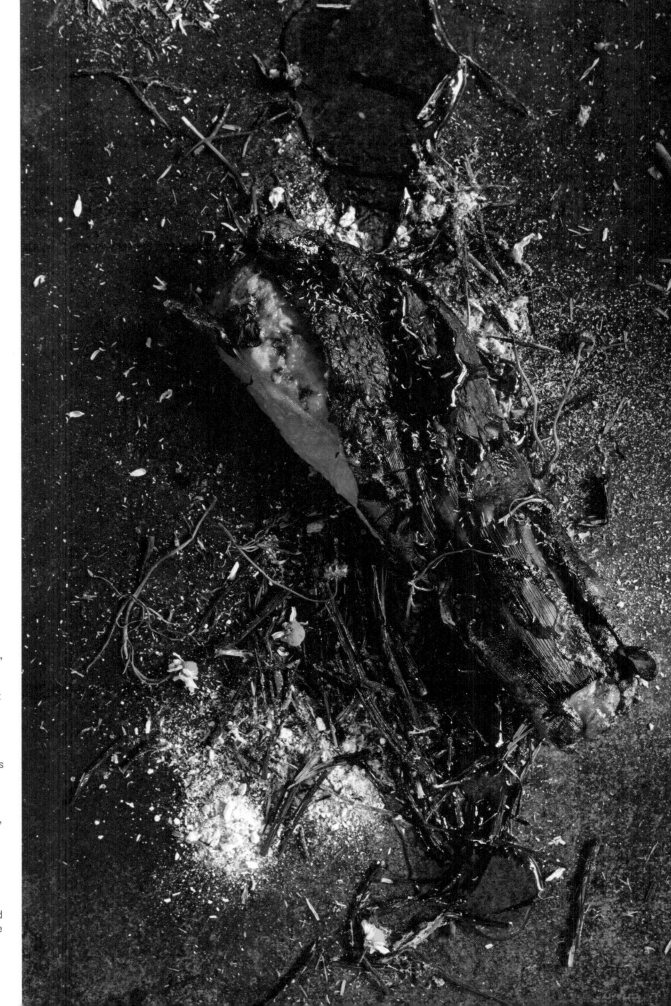

On our chalkboard menu, the side dishes that we offer might not look like anything special—sweet potatoes, plátanos, beets, and yuca can sound pretty boring—but the wood-burning oven does magical things to even the most basic ingredients. The intense heat brings out the sweetness in everything, and that caramely concentration and char are transformative. Depending on the side, we'll finish it with a drizzle of honey, a knob of butter, a pinch of dried chamomile, or a crumble of dried avocado leaves. Even a simple dish can be multidimensional.

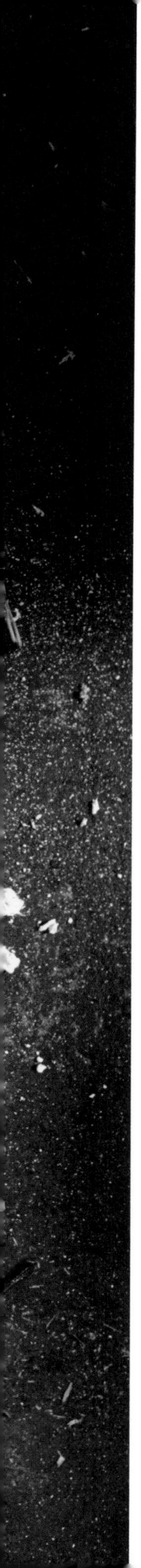

The bananas that we blister in the wood-burning oven until they get soft and sweet and custardy are called plátanos machos (Spanish for "big bananas"). We buy them when still firm and hang them in the kitchen until the skin is dark brown, even a little black in places. You can find large cooking bananas at any Mexican grocery and at many specialty markets—you might be able to find them at a regular supermarket—and if you do, let them get as ripe as possible before trying this recipe. If you can't find plátanos machos, substitute super-ripe conventional bananas. The blistered plátanos make a good side dish for skirt steak, pork ribs, or pork belly, or even the grilled fish. SERVES 6

BLISTERED PLÁTANOS with HONEY

6 large ripe plátanos

1 cinnamon stick

1 tablespoon dried chamomile or chamomile tea (preferably organic)

3 tablespoons dark honey

Preheat the oven as high as it will go, at least 500°F.

Put the plátanos in a roasting pan and roast for 20 minutes, or until the skin starts to split and some of the flesh oozes out.

Transfer the plátanos to plates and use the tip of a sharp knife to split them open, then squeeze the ends so that the flesh is pushed out of the charred peel. Finish each serving with a grating of cinnamon (use a Microplane), a pinch of crumbled chamomile, and a drizzle of honey.

We keep stalks of sugarcane in a galvanized bucket on the table in front of the wood-burning stove, using them to flavor a roast the way other restaurants might use a few sprigs of thyme or rosemary. We split open a piece and throw it into the pan to highlight whatever natural sweetness will be brought out by the fire. When we get a delivery of sugarcane, we hack the long stalks in 2-foot pieces with a machete; you might be able to find smaller pieces in a Mexican grocery or even at Whole Foods. SERVES 4

ROASTED BEETS with AVOCADO-HABANERO CREMA

BEETS

4 large beets, scrubbed

One 6-inch piece sugarcane, split in half (optional)

8 basil sprigs

Olive oil for drizzling

Kosher salt and freshly ground black pepper

Ground allspice

AVOCADO-HABANERO CREMA

1 ripe Hass avocado, halved, pitted, and peeled

½ habanero, seeded (leave the seeds in if you want a hotter sauce)

1 cup sour cream

¼ cup olive oil

½ teaspoon honey

1 teaspoon kosher salt, or to taste

½ teaspoon freshly ground black pepper, or to taste

Chile Lime Salt, for garnish

Preheat the oven to 375°F.

Put the beets, sugarcane, if using, and basil in a baking dish and fill about one-third full with water. Cover tightly with aluminum foil and bake for 45 to 60 minutes, until a knife pierces all the way through a beet easily. Remove the beets from the liquid and let cool slightly. Increase the oven temperature to 425°F.

Meanwhile, make the avocado-habanero crema: Combine all the ingredients in a blender and blend on high for about 10 seconds. Turn off the blender and scrape down the sides with a rubber spatula to make sure everything gets a turn. Repeat until a smooth cream forms—this will take more than a few tries. Season to taste if necessary. Transfer to a bowl, cover, and refrigerate for about 30 minutes, or until ready to serve.

Cut the beets in half and place in a large cast-iron skillet. Drizzle with olive oil and sprinkle with salt and pepper. Roast for 15 to 20 minutes, until the beets are hot all the way though and the ends have started to crisp up.

Serve the beets topped with the crema, dusted with allspice and chile lime salt.

CHILE LIME SALT

MAKES ABOUT 2 TABLESPOONS

Our version of a finishing salt, this brings a note of intrigue to any dish. It's simple to make: Toast dried árbol chiles in a cast-iron pan, pulverize them in a spice grinder, and mix in lime zest and salt. That's it. The smoky, spicy, tangy salt is just the right flourish for grilled fish, but you can use it in or on just about any dish. We sprinkle it over the odd-shaped pieces left over when we make jicama salad, or you could use it on radishes or eggs.

4 dried árbol chiles   Grated zest of 3 limes

2 tablespoons kosher salt

Toast the chiles in a dry cast-iron skillet over medium-low heat until fragrant, about 2 minutes. Let cool. Pulse the chiles in a spice grinder to a fine powder. Mix with the salt and lime zest. Store in a tightly sealed jar in a cool place.

You treat yuca like a potato: peel it, trim it into pieces, drop into salted boiling water, and cook until soft, then drain and mash. The tricky part is removing the skin, a thick, bark-like exterior with a thin but tough underlayer. You need to use a heavy chef's knife and put some muscle into it (and even then you might not be able to cut through the area closest to the stem; move the blade until you locate a spot where you can). Yuca can be long, so the best thing is to first trim it down into manageable pieces: cut the yuca into 3-inch-long sections, then stand them on end on the cutting board so that you can use your body weight to help you cut off the skin. SERVES 4

CREAMED YUCA

Kosher salt

2 large yuca, peeled

1 large shallot, minced

2 tablespoons mashed Roasted Garlic (page 62), plus 4 roasted garlic cloves for garnish

2 tablespoons Roasted Garlic Oil (page 62) or olive oil

Freshly ground black pepper

½ cup heavy cream

Fill a large saucepan with water, add 1 tablespoon salt, and bring to a boil. Using a chef's knife, cut the yuca into 3-inch lengths as directed above, then cut the sections into 1-inch disks. Add to the boiling water and cook until tender, 15 to 30 minutes. The yuca will release a thick, starchy film, but fear not—that's what's going to give it that creamy texture once you mash it. Drain.

Transfer the yuca to a large bowl, add the shallot, roasted garlic, and roasted garlic oil, and mash with a heavy wooden spoon—you want most of the yuca to fall apart, but there should still be some small chunks. Add pepper to taste and more salt if necessary. Add the cream and stir to incorporate, then taste and adjust the seasoning again if needed. Serve topped with the roasted garlic cloves.

SILENCE & SOLITUDE

When we first came to the Yucatán, we often found ourselves in large spaces that were totally silent. The roads here can be so straight that you need to force yourself to stay awake at the wheel, but the land that you can't see from your car contains families, farms, and settlements. At first it seems like there's nothing there, just a wall of green, but then you start to notice gaps in the wall of plants marked by poles with something distinctive hanging off the end: a rag, a tire, a plastic bottle dipped in paint. These mark the paths that thread through the jungle, an unofficial transportation network that connects the roads to the hundreds of thousands of acres of land in active use. When you drive out to a farm, parking the truck once the suspension can no longer handle the rutted path and proceeding on foot, you might find yourself in a space so big and quiet that when you see the farmer, it's as if the two of you are experiencing the solitude together.

It's easy to say we moved here for the incredible markets and the climate, but that's just the surface. It was only later that we truly realized why we're in the Yucatán. It was to see one world after another open up to us, and to understand that no matter how much is going on in your life at that moment, your troubles are small when thrown into the vast scale of what's out there. That's when you can be free from the mist that fogs up your mind, or the darkness that you hold onto even though you don't mean to, because it's easier than confronting yourself. The space makes you stronger and makes you simplify what you do.

It is incredible what can grow from the smallest amount of light. This window to the sky from a cenote far below the surface allows a canopy full of life to take over. Walking through the jungle on a path taken daily makes one feel humble and grateful. So much exciting wildness makes you understand how much you have to learn.

We get spring onions year-round—it's always spring in the Yucatán—and after a quick charring, they're the perfect accompaniment for grilled lamb, grouper, or really just about any meat or fish that comes off the grill or out of the oven. The recipe is simple, but the roasted garlic oil and a little sprinkle of ground guajillo chile builds flavor. We use the youngest spring onions we can get, so the bulbs are about the size of a cherry tomato.   SERVES 2

CHARRED SPRING ONIONS

1 bunch spring onions, trimmed, rinsed, and patted dry

3 tablespoons Roasted Garlic Oil (page 62)

1 small dried guajillo chile, toasted in a dry skillet until fragrant and ground in a spice grinder

Kosher salt and freshly ground black pepper

Preheat the oven to 400°F.

Rub the onions with some of the garlic oil and arrange in a large cast-iron skillet. Season with the chile and salt and pepper to taste. Roast for 25 minutes, basting the onions with more oil every 5 minutes, until the bulbs are soft and the outer layer is charred.

Tomatillos, which look like small green tomatoes, are actually related to the gooseberry and cook down into a tangy, pulpy liquid. Although tomatillo salsa is one of the standards of Mexican cooking, it is almost never a part of a dish on the menu at Hartwood, to be honest. Instead, it plays an important role in our family meals—what we cook for ourselves. Because we always have the oven and grill going, we roast tomatillos with red onions and chiles and add some roasted garlic from our garlic oil, along with cilantro and lime juice. We use the sauce for the fish tacos we make for family meal, or with the *chilaquiles con pollo y huevo* we fry up with leftover tortillas.

MAKES ABOUT 4 CUPS

TOMATILLO SALSA

8 tomatillos, husks removed, rinsed, patted dry, and halved

1 small red onion, thinly sliced

1 tablespoon mashed Roasted Garlic (page 62)

½ jalapeño

2 teaspoons coriander seeds

1 teaspoon cumin seeds

1 tablespoon kosher salt, plus more to taste

1 teaspoon freshly ground black pepper, plus more to taste

2 tablespoons olive oil

1 teaspoon honey

2 cups cilantro leaves

¼ cup water

½ cup fresh lime juice (from 5 to 6 limes)

Preheat the oven to 400°F.

Combine the tomatillos, onion, roasted garlic, jalapeño, coriander, cumin, salt, pepper, and olive oil in a baking dish and mix well. Roast for about 20 minutes, or until the vegetables start to char, turning them occasionally so that the spices don't burn. Remove from the oven and let cool.

Transfer the vegetables to a blender, along with any roasting juices. Add the honey, cilantro, and water, and blend on high speed until smooth, about 2 minutes. Add the lime juice and salt and pepper to taste.

El Mar

THE SEA

The best time for fish is April through June. We always have beautiful fish here—we get red snapper and grouper year-round. But in the late spring we start getting jack crevalle, dorado, Spanish mackerel, bluefin tuna, and both white and blue marlin. That's when we get a type of red snapper called a rainbow runner that's just spectacular. But the favorite fish here is wahoo, which we first see in April and which are gone in June. The fish is rich and fatty and a little bit oily. When you make it into a ceviche, it melts in your mouth like a really good piece of sushi.

The big fish return to the waters here because they're following schools of smaller fish. You can tell when the little ones are back by looking in the sky for a kind of black tern known as a man-o'-war, which feeds on the schools. The fishermen don't need sonar or GPS to find the big fish, they just track the man-o'-wars and set out in their boats.

EL CEVICHE
DEL DIAS

There's always at least one ceviche on the menu at Hartwood. The fish we get is so exceptional that it could be used in a sushi restaurant, but ceviche is refreshing, and it's a great way to play with Mexican ingredients. Citrus and chiles is a magical combination of flavors

The recipes here reflect what we put on the menu, with the fish that we have access to in this part of the Caribbean. Maybe you can't find the fish called for, or you can but it looks tired and not right for ceviche. So: don't do it. Instead use the freshest, best-quality fish you can get. The ginger and mezcal in the ceviche liquid for marlin could be used for most firm-fleshed fish, such as grouper, swordfish, bass, amberjack, rockfish, tilefish, and Atlantic perch. You want a fish that can stand up to those strong flavors. The grapefruit, mandarin, and lime juices with honey that we use for wahoo make good partners for just about any medium-fleshed fish: striped bass in the Northeast, red snapper on the Pacific Coast, river or lake trout in the Midwest.

Your best plan of action is to read through the recipes, then go to the market and pick a fish. Once you do that, you can decide which ceviche is right for what you bought. It's what we do at Hartwood: When the fishermen stop by the restaurant with the day's catch, we don't ask them for a particular fish; we look at what's best, then we start prepping the ceviche. Buy whole fish if you can. If you break down the fish yourself, you can keep the flesh closer to pristine for as long as possible.

The ceviches we make don't sit around all day. Instead, they call for a quick toss with sweet lime and other citrus juices to cure and lightly marinate. (Ceviche doesn't actually "cook" the flesh, but the effect is similar.) Really, you're delicately tossing raw fish with a dressing, and you want that fish to be in perfect condition.

The earthy, smoky flavor of the mezcal sets up both the sharpness of the citrus in the marinade and the fattiness of the avocado. When shopping for marlin, look for a lean fillet with no fatty layers between the muscle—that fat is too chewy for a ceviche. If you can't find lean marlin, ask for lean swordfish. If the only marlin (or swordfish) at the fish market is fatty, then don't make ceviche: those cuts are best roasted in the oven.   SERVES 4 TO 6

CEVICHE de AGUJA with GINGER and MEZCAL

GINGER MEZCAL AGUA

½ cup thinly sliced ginger

½ cup fresh lime juice (from 5 to 6 limes)

1 cucumber, peeled and cut into chunks

2 tablespoons mezcal

½ teaspoon honey

1 serrano chile, coarsely chopped

⅓ cup dried chamomile or organic chamomile tea

Kosher salt

CEVICHE

1 pound marlin fillets, cut into ¼-inch-thick slices (see How to Slice for Ceviche, page 120)

½ teaspoon kosher salt

⅓ cup Pickled White Onions (page 54)

4 radishes, julienned

1 serrano chile, thinly sliced

⅓ cup ½-inch cubes seeded cucumber

¼ cup hoja santa leaves, cut into ½-inch squares (optional)

1 Hass avocado, halved, pitted, peeled, and cubed

½ teaspoon dried chamomile or organic chamomile tea for garnish

Radish sprouts for garnish (optional)

Sea salt for garnish

Make the ginger mezcal agua: Combine the ginger, lime juice, cucumber, mezcal, honey, serrano, and chamomile in a blender and blend on high for about 30 seconds, until well blended. Pass through a fine-mesh strainer into a bowl and add salt to taste.

Put the marlin in a bowl, add the ginger mezcal agua and salt, and gently mix to combine. Add the pickled white onions, radishes, serrano, cucumber, and hoja santa, if using, and mix gently. Let stand for 1 to 2 minutes.

Using a slotted spoon, divide the ceviche among individual serving bowls. Spoon about 2 tablespoons of the ginger mezcal agua over each serving. Garnish with the avocado, chamomile, radish sprouts, if using, and sea salt.

HOW TO SLICE FOR CEVICHE

When you cut fish for ceviche, angle your knife at 45 degrees and make thin cuts against the grain so that each piece is about ¼-inch thick. Make sure that you are slicing in one fluid movement—it's like slicing through an apple, not sawing though a loaf of bread. Be mindful that the grain might change as you move along the fish, so be sure to adjust the angle of your cut accordingly. Take your time. You're making ceviche for you and your friends, not trying to beat the clock.

At Hartwood, we slice tuna loin into lengths and sprinkle with salt and chamomile for a quick cure before cutting into thin slices for ceviche.

Be sure to serve this dish in shallow bowls: everyone will want to drink the super–vegetal broth after they've finished the fish.   SERVES 4 TO 6

CEVICHE de ATÚN with RUBY RED LECHE DE TIGRE

1 pound tuna steaks, skin removed

2 tablespoons kosher salt

½ cup dried chamomile or organic chamomile tea (or dried herb of choice, such as basil or oregano)

LECHE DE TIGRE

1 carrot, peeled and cut into 1–inch pieces

1 cucumber, peeled and cut into 1–inch pieces

1 small beet, peeled and cut into 1–inch pieces

1 small red onion, cut into ½–inch–thick slices

3 tomatoes, cut into 2–inch pieces

1 serrano chile

¼ cup fresh lime juice (from 2 to 3 limes)

2 cups coconut water, or more to taste

¾ cup fresh grapefruit juice

Kosher salt

GARNISHES

1 Hass avocado, halved, pitted, peeled, and thinly sliced

1 grapefruit, suprêmed (see page 45)

½ cup diced peeled, seeded cucumber

2 radishes, julienned

1 jalapeño, thinly sliced

Dried chamomile

Trim away the deep purple blood line that runs through the tuna to remove as much of the iron-tasting blood as you can. Sprinkle with the salt and chamomile, put in an airtight container, and refrigerate for 30 to 45 minutes.

Make the leche de tigre: Pass the carrot, cucumber, beet, red onion, tomatoes, and serrano through a juicer. (Alternatively, use a blender: Put the carrot, cucumber, beet, onion, tomatoes, serrano, lime juice, and half the coconut water in a blender and blend on high speed until liquefied, 1 to 2 minutes. Strain through a fine-mesh sieve; discard the solids.)

Combine the vegetable liquid, lime juice (unless you used a blender), grapefruit juice, and (the remaining) coconut water in a bowl and mix well. Add salt to taste. (If the mixture is too spicy, add more coconut water.) Set aside.

Rinse the tuna to remove the chamomile and salt and pat dry with paper towels. Angle your knife at 45 degrees and make thin ¼–inch–thick cuts against the grain. Be careful to make one fluid cut for each slice; cutting in a sawing motion will destroy the flesh. Put the slices in a medium bowl and add the leche de tigre, turning to coat.

Remove the tuna slices from the liquid and divide among individual serving bowls. Spoon enough leche de tigre onto each plate to just cover the bottom of the bowl. Garnish with the avocado, grapefruit, cucumber, radishes, jalapeño, and dried chamomile.

How do you give a ceviche marinade more body so that it holds onto the fish and has some structure on the plate? The creamy, fragrant flesh of the saramuyo, or custard apple, has some structure, so that the marinade doesn't just turn into a puddle. The saramuyo also adds an undertone of sweetness while allowing the lime and salt to cut through and zap your taste buds.

You can use any firm white-fleshed fish for this recipe. It works especially well with snapper and striped bass. **SERVES 4 TO 6**

CEVICHE de JUREL with SARAMUYO and COCONUT WATER

1 cup thinly sliced star fruit

1 teaspoon sugar, or to taste

1 pound jurel fillets, cut into ¼-inch-thick slices (see How to Slice for Ceviche, page 120)

1 teaspoon kosher salt, plus more to taste

¼ cup thinly sliced red onion

½ cup cubed dragon fruit flesh (or substitute fresh coconut meat)

2 tablespoons thinly sliced jalapeño

2 tablespoons cilantro leaves

2 tablespoons basil leaves

2 tablespoons mint leaves

2 tablespoons amaranth leaves, cut into squares (optional)

1 cup Saramuyo Salsa

Sea salt

Olive oil for drizzling

Put the star fruit in a small bowl and sprinkle with the sugar. Toss and set aside for 10 minutes to cure and allow excess water to seep out. (Star fruit is slightly acidic, so you want to keep some of that along with the sweetness, but taste and use a bit more sugar if necessary.)

Put the jurel slices in a large bowl and sprinkle with the salt. Add the red onion, star fruit, dragon fruit, jalapeño, cilantro, basil, mint, and amaranth, if using. Then add the saramuyo salsa and mix gently with your hands. Season to taste with more salt as needed.

Divide the ceviche among small serving bowls and sprinkle with sea salt. Drizzle lightly with olive oil.

SARAMUYO SALSA

MAKES ABOUT 1 CUP

2 ripe saramuyo (or cherimoyas)

½ cup coconut water

2 tablespoons unsweetened coconut cream (the thick liquid at the top of the can of coconut milk)

2 tablespoons fresh lime juice

1 teaspoon kosher salt, or to taste

Halve the saramuyo and scoop out the pulp, seeds and all. Put it into a blender, add the coconut water, and blend on high for 20 to 30 seconds.

Pour the puree through a fine-mesh strainer into a bowl. Stir in the coconut cream, lime juice, and salt. Refrigerate until ready to use.

THE ICE BRIGADE

Every day at around noon, we get a delivery of fifty or so bags and blocks of ice. Some days Juan brings it in his taxi, other days one of our suppliers will stop by the ice plant in town. Some of the ice goes to the bar to cool down beers and wine in time for dinner, but most of it is used to replenish the twelve massive ice chests we have out back and the three we keep to one side of the kitchen.

Most of our refrigeration is done with ice and ice chests. We do have a refrigerator and a freezer that we power with batteries (fed by the solar panels on the roof and by a judiciously short run of the gas generator), but these are not big appliances—they have about the same capacity as what you'd find in an American home. If we bought more refrigeration, we would need more power. And even so, there's no guarantee they would work. The jungle air is hard on machines, as is the sea air. On numerous occasions, we have arrived in the morning to find that the refrigerator was running hot, or malfunctioning, or not running at all.

The fish we get is so magnificent that we want to be sure to handle it as carefully as we can. Fresh ice is the way to go. You can count on ice chests filled with ice to keep things cold. In fact, they are good at keeping things cold even when it is scorching hot outside—they function better than any home refrigerator, and if you do it right, they stay as frigid as a top-of-the-line professional walk-in. One of the keys is to open them as little as possible.

The noon ice run is the first of three. There's another delivery around 4:30, just before the restaurant opens. This is the ice that we'll use for the drinks in the bar and for the water glasses on the table, though some of the ice goes into the chests as well. Then we'll get a final top-up delivery around 10:30, just before we close, to keep everything in the ice chests cool until the first delivery the next day.

Robalo wanders in and out of fresh and saltwater like a lagoon vagabond. It's very difficult to catch, which is why it's wickedly expensive and considered a delicacy. You need a spear. You need a guide.

Ceviche is the ideal preparation for this valuable fish because it's all about minimal intrusion. The fresh citrus juice and salt gently cure the robalo, with its lovely texture, and the coconut water and cucumber juice balance the salt and lime juice so all you taste is the bright fish.

Any firm, moist white fish—such as grouper—works well too.   SERVES 4 TO 6

CEVICHE de ROBALO

1 pound skinned robalo fillet, cut into ¼-inch-thick slices (see How to Slice for Ceviche, page 120)

2 cups fresh orange juice (from 5 to 6 oranges)

1 cup fresh lime juice (from 10 to 12 limes)

1 red onion, diced

1 red serrano chile, thinly sliced

½ teaspoon kosher salt

2 cups coconut water

1 cup cucumber juice (see Note)

1 grapefruit, suprêmed (see page 45)

¼ jicama, peeled and cut into batons

2 radishes, cut into batons

1 cucumber, peeled, halved lengthwise, seeded, and cut into small cubes

1 cup opal basil leaves (or regular basil)

1 Hass avocado, halved, pitted, peeled, and cut into thin slices or small cubes

Sea salt

Put the fish in a bowl or other nonreactive container and add the orange juice, lime juice, red onion, serrano, and salt. Cover and refrigerate for at least 30 minutes, and up to 1 hour.

To serve, using a slotted spoon, place a scoop of the ceviche in each serving dish. Combine the coconut water and cucumber juice and ladle into the bowls. Garnish with the grapefruit, jicama, radishes, cucumber, basil leaves, and avocado. Finish each with a pinch of sea salt.

Note: You will need about 2 cucumbers to yield 1 cup juice. Peel, cut into chunks, and blend until pureed, then strain.

The wahoo start running in April but don't really take off until May, when Tulum is sweltering—which is why this ceviche is a bright mixture of three kinds of fresh citrus juice: grapefruit, mandarin orange, and lime. We serve it as cold as possible, so that it refreshes as it feeds you. Think of it almost as a palate cleanser for the summer heat. The wahoo are bountiful through the first week in June, then fade away until the next year. This dish follows the fish, disappearing until they return.

If you can't get wahoo, you can substitute other very fresh mackerel.

SERVES 4 TO 6

CEVICHE de WAHOO with PINK GRAPEFRUIT

1 cup fresh pink grapefruit juice

½ cup fresh mandarin orange juice (or substitute regular orange juice)

¼ cup fresh lime juice (from 2 to 3 limes)

1 teaspoon honey

1 teaspoon kosher salt, or to taste

1 pound wahoo fillets, trimmed and cut into ¼-inch-thick slices (see How to Slice for Ceviche, page 120)

1 pink grapefruit, suprêmed (see page 45)

1 cup cherry tomatoes, halved

¼ cup Pickled White or Red Onions (page 54)

½ serrano chile, thinly sliced

16 green basil leaves

16 purple basil leaves (or additional regular basil)

16 mint leaves

Mix together the grapefruit juice, orange juice, lime juice, honey, and salt in a bowl and stir with a spoon or whisk to blend. Add the wahoo, toss lightly to coat, and refrigerate for 15 to 20 minutes.

Add the grapefruit suprêmes, tomatoes, pickled onions, serrano, basil, and mint to the wahoo and toss well. Taste and adjust the seasoning.

Divide the ceviche among four small bowls. Serve immediately.

This bright yellow church has stood
in Oxkutzcab for hundreds of years,
reminding us that color can be timeless yet
new—a thought that inspires our cooking.

In case you're wondering, fish dip is not a Mexican dish. It's purely an American thing, but it's one of those standards that deserves a second look. You can use any fish you want—the oilier the better. We make this with sierra, or Spanish mackerel.

This first went on the menu as something that people could order right away to have with drinks. It also prepares diners for more fish—we're big fans of surf-'n-surf. And if it seems surprising that we use Chardonnay in the guajillo caper sauce, it's not: the vineyards around Baja produce some great whites that can stand up to the herbs and chiles in the complex, creamy sauce.

We serve this dip with homemade flatbreads, but you can use tostadas or tortilla chips instead. Huayas look like little limes, but they crack open to reveal a lychee–like pinkish–orange fruit with sweet–tart flesh surrounding a large seed. They make a fun garnish but are completely optional.

SERVES 6 TO 8

SIERRA DIP with GUAJILLO CHILE FLATBREADS

1 pound sierra (Spanish mackerel) fillets

½ cup olive oil

1 tablespoon kosher salt

1½ teaspoons freshly ground black pepper

1 orange, cut into ½-inch-thick slices (peel and all)

Guajillo Caper Sauce

1½ teaspoons Chile Lime Salt (page 100)

Huaya, peeled, for garnish (optional)

Guajillo Chile Flatbreads (recipe follows)

Preheat the oven to 350°F.

Put the mackerel in a baking dish and add the olive oil, turning to coat. Season on both sides with the salt and pepper. Place the orange slices on top and bake for about 30 minutes, or until the fish is cooked through. Remove from the heat and let cool.

Drain the fish; remove any skin and remaining bones and finely flake by hand into a bowl. Add the guajillo caper sauce and mix until thoroughly combined. (The dip can be made a day ahead and refrigerated. Serve at room temperature.)

To serve, garnish the dip with the chile lime salt and huaya and serve with the flatbread.

GUAJILLO CAPER SAUCE

MAKES ABOUT 1 CUP

1 dried guajillo chile, stems and seeds removed

1 teaspoon coriander seeds

¼ teaspoon cumin seeds

¼ teaspoon black peppercorns

⅓ cup Chardonnay

¼ cup water

2½ tablespoons white vinegar

1 tarragon sprig

1 oregano sprig

¼ carrot, peeled

1½ teaspoons capers

¼ cup olive oil

2½ tablespoons sour cream

Combine all the ingredients except the capers, olive oil, and sour cream in a medium saucepan. Bring to a simmer over medium heat and simmer until the mixture is reduced to a third of its original volume, about 10 minutes. Let cool, then remove the tarragon, oregano, and carrot.

Add the mixture to a blender, along with the capers, and blend on high speed until smooth, about 1 minute. Slowly add the olive oil, blending until incorporated. Add the sour cream and blend until smooth. Refrigerate until ready to serve.

GUAJILLO CHILE FLATBREADS

MAKES ABOUT 16 FLATBREADS

4 dried guajillo chiles, seeds and stems removed

2 cups water

2½ cups all-purpose flour

1 teaspoon kosher salt

¼ cup olive oil

Put the chiles in a small saucepan, add the water, bring to a boil, and cook until the chiles are soft, about 5 minutes. Drain, reserving the cooking water.

Put the chiles in a blender, along with 1 cup of the cooking water and blend until smooth, about 20 seconds.

Combine the flour, salt, oil, and blendered chiles in a large bowl and mix using a wooden spoon or your hands, until a rough dough forms. Transfer the dough to a floured surface and set the bowl aside. Knead the dough until smooth, about 15 minutes; it will be slightly wet and tacky, so flour the work surface as you need to prevent sticking. Return the dough to the bowl, cover, and let sit for 10 to 20 minutes.

Divide the dough into 16 pieces and roll into small balls.

Prepare a grill for medium heat or preheat a large dry cast-iron skillet over medium-high heat. Roll out several balls of dough on a floured surface to about ⅛ inch thick. Place on the grill or in the skillet. Once you see the dough stiffen and bubbles start to rise, about 1 minute, take a look underneath: it should be lightly browned in spots. Flip and cook on the other side, about 1 minute more. Transfer to a napkin-lined basket to keep warm. Repeat with the remaining dough.

Here's the secret about octopus: the more times you cook it, the better it is. Everything in this dish gets cooked two ways for extra levels of crispness, reflecting how we move from wood–burning oven to grill at Hartwood.

The combination of infused oils and the floral coriander dressing add layers of flavor that will convince you that you really do need to keep roasted onion oil *and* roasted chile oil on hand, not to mention roasted garlic.

Octopus are sold whole. We use only the tentacles of the octopus for this dish (and save the head for family–meal tacos) because we feel the meaty tentacles are best suited for the grill, but that can make shopping complicated. You can use the whole octopus, or you can up how much you buy and only use the tentacles. Just save the heads for tacos. You will have to buy several small, or one medium octopus for this dish and cut the tentacles off the heads.   SERVES 4

PULPO ASADO with ROASTED POTATOES and CORIANDER DRESSING

OCTOPUS

3 thyme sprigs

3 oregano sprigs

2 pounds octopus tentacles

6 tablespoons Roasted Chile Oil
(page 63)

6 tablespoons Roasted Garlic Oil
(page 62)

VEGETABLES

16 new potatoes, halved

½ cup Roasted Onion Oil (page 64)

Kosher salt and freshly ground
black pepper

8 xctatic chiles or 2 to 3 habaneros,
roughly chopped

2 white onions, halved lengthwise and
thinly sliced crosswise

¼ cup Roasted Chile Oil (page 63)

1 tablespoon mashed Roasted Garlic
(page 62)

CORIANDER DRESSING

1 tablespoon coriander seeds, toasted
in a dry skillet until fragrant, and
finely ground

¼ cup cilantro leaves

1 teaspoon mashed Roasted Garlic
(page 62)

½ shallot, minced

½ teaspoon honey

½ cup olive oil

½ teaspoon kosher salt, or to taste

Freshly ground black pepper to taste

1 bunch mustard greens, sliced into
2-inch pieces

2 limes, halved

Pickled Red Onions (page 54) for
garnish (optional)

Prepare the octopus: Fill a large pot with water, season generously with salt, add the herb sprigs, and bring to a boil. While the water heats, pound the octopus tentacles with a heavy blunt object for a minute or so to tenderize (a small cast-iron skillet would work for this; we use a log).

Add the octopus tentacles to the boiling water and boil for about 45 minutes, or until they are tender and a toothpick is easily inserted in the flesh. Transfer to a bowl of ice water to stop the cooking.

Once the octopus tentacles have cooled completely, drain, seal in a plastic bag, and refrigerate (this gives the meat a chance to firm up before you grill it).

Prepare the vegetables: Preheat the oven to 400°F.

Put the potatoes in a large cast-iron skillet with ¼ cup of the roasted onion oil and toss to coat. Add salt and pepper to taste and toss again. Roast for 15 to 20 minutes, or until the potatoes are tender on the inside and crispy on the outside. Transfer the potatoes to a bowl; set the skillet aside for the moment. Reduce the oven temperature to 350°F.

Put the chiles and white onions in the hot skillet, add the chile oil and roasted garlic, and toss to coat. Add salt and pepper to taste and toss again. Roast for 30 minutes, or until crisped and tender. Remove from the heat and set aside in the skillet.

Meanwhile, make the coriander dressing: Whisk together all the ingredients in a small bowl until combined. Taste and season again if necessary.

Prepare a grill for high heat.

Preheat the broiler. Add the roast potatoes to the skillet with the chiles and onions and toss with the remaining ¼ cup onion oil. Broil for 10 minutes, or until the vegetables are very crispy. Remove from the heat.

Toss the octopus tentacles with the 6 tablespoons of roasted chile oil and the 6 tablespoons of roasted garlic oil. Oil the grill grate, then grill the octopus tentacles on one side until crispy, about 2 minutes. Flip and repeat on the other side.

To serve, toss the mustard greens with ¼ cup of the coriander dressing and arrange on four serving plates. Pile the roasted potatoes, chiles, and onions on the greens. Lightly coat the octopus with the remaining coriander dressing and place atop the vegetables. Garnish each plate with half a lime and the pickled red onions, if using.

This old fishing boat that came ashore along Soliman Bay is now home to pelicans and other seabirds. Charlie, our daughter, likes to play around it. There are many places to find a moment of peace with family and friends along the beaches of Tulum.

It's easy to put calamar on the menu of a restaurant by the beach—bread it, fry it, and serve it with a dipping sauce, and watch it fly out of the kitchen. But we wanted a dish that reflected local ingredients, so we serve it with a sauce made with zapote negro, a tropical fruit that has soft, dark flesh that tastes like fermented molasses. The sauce anchors the calamar, giving it an earthy flavor.

The secret to calamar is to grill it over a high flame that will quickly cook off the water content of the flesh (use a medium flame, and it will be gummy instead of charred). If your flame is powerful enough, one minute on either side is all you need.

If you can't find zapote negro at a specialty produce market, you can substitute prunes simmered in water until they plump up. Or you can skip the sauce, grill the calamar, toss it with the salad and basil dressing, and call it a day.   SERVES 6 TO 8

GRILLED CALAMAR SALAD

CHICKPEA SALAD

2 cups dried chickpeas, soaked overnight in cold water to cover

1 white onion

1 carrot

7 thyme sprigs

7 oregano sprigs

3 bay leaves

1 Burnt Onion (page 64)

2 cups heirloom cherry tomatoes, halved

½ pound spinach, washed and torn into pieces

2 radishes, thinly sliced

1 lime, suprêmed (see page 45)

½ cup purple or green basil leaves

Kosher salt and freshly ground black pepper

Make the chickpeas: Combine the chickpeas, onion, carrot, thyme, oregano, and bay leaves in a large saucepan. Add water to cover by several inches and bring to a simmer over low heat, then simmer until the chickpeas are tender, 25 to 40 minutes. Drain, discard the bay leaves, herb sprigs, onion, and carrot, and transfer to a large bowl.

Meanwhile, make the dressing: Put all the ingredients in a blender and puree until smooth, about 30 seconds. Set aside.

Make the sauce: If using prunes, put them in a small saucepan with 1 cup water and simmer until they have plumped and feel slightly squishy to the touch, 15 to 20 minutes. If using zapote, halve the fruit, remove the seeds, and scoop out the flesh.

Toast the sunflower seeds, chiles, and cacao nibs in a small dry skillet until fragrant. Let cool, then grind in a spice grinder.

Put the zapote (or prunes), ground chile mixture, and all the remaining sauce ingredients in a blender and puree until smooth, about 30 seconds. Transfer to a bowl.

Make the calamar: Prepare a grill for high heat.

Meanwhile, toast the allspice and black peppercorns in a small dry skillet over medium heat until fragrant, then grind in a spice grinder.

Season the calamar with the ground spices and salt and toss with ½ cup of the olive oil. Grill the calamar until marked on both sides and charred and just opaque throughout, 1 to 2 minutes per side. Let cool.

Just before serving, add the burnt onion, tomatoes, spinach, radishes, lime, and basil to the chickpeas and toss well. Season with salt and pepper, add the dressing, and toss again.

Slice the calamar into ¼-inch-wide rings and toss with the lime juice and the remaining ½ cup olive oil.

To serve, smear 2 tablespoons of the zapote negro sauce across each plate. Arrange the salad on top and then top with the calamar.

BASIL ONION DRESSING

½ cup Roasted Onion Oil (page 64)

1½ teaspoons fresh lime juice

1 cup packed basil leaves

1½ teaspoons kosher salt

1½ teaspoons freshly ground black pepper

ZAPOTE NEGRO SAUCE

1 ripe zapote negro (or substitute 3 or 4 prunes)

2 tablespoons sunflower seeds

1 dried guajillo chile

2 dried árbol chiles

1 teaspoon cacao nibs

2 tablespoons tamarind pulp

2 tablespoons honey

1 tablespoon fresh lime juice

½ cup water

½ teaspoon finely ground coffee beans

Generous pinch of ground cinnamon

½ teaspoon kosher salt

CALAMAR

1½ pounds cleaned calamar (squid) bodies

1 teaspoon allspice berries

1 teaspoon black peppercorns

1 teaspoon kosher salt

1 cup olive oil

¼ cup fresh lime juice (from 2 to 3 limes)

This dish started off as a family meal, when we took the heads left over from the day's pulpo asado. After boiling them, we tossed the heads with a dressing (instead of grilling them like the tentacles), then piled them on fried tortillas. We refined the dish before we put it on the menu: the tostadas are freshly made, the octopus is from the more delicious tentacles, and the dressing is more precise and flavorful. It's a simple dish that we dolled up.

Sometimes we make the masa ourselves (see page 210), and sometimes we buy it from vendors in town. If you can, buy fresh masa from a restaurant or tortilla manufacturer willing to part with some. If not, you can make tortillas with just dried Maseca (corn flour) according to the package directions. As a last resort, buy fresh tortillas. You don't want to drive yourself crazy chasing after authenticity, but the better the masa, the more flavorful the dish—you don't need to bake bread to make a sandwich, but a sandwich made with just-baked bread tastes so much better than one made with bagged stuff from a supermarket. SERVES 6

PULPO TOSTADAS

1 pound new potatoes (6 to 8, depending on size)

TOSTADAS

Olive oil for frying

12 freshly made corn tortillas, homemade (see page 210) or store-bought

VINAIGRETTE

1 tablespoon mashed Roasted Garlic (page 62)

2 tablespoons fresh lime juice

½ cup olive oil

1 teaspoon honey

½ teaspoon kosher salt, or to taste

1 teaspoon freshly ground black pepper

1 tablespoon finely diced red onion

2 cups thinly sliced cooked octopus (about 1 pound; follow the boiling instructions in the recipe on page 137)

½ cup finely chopped heirloom tomatoes

4 radishes, thinly sliced

¼ cup cucumber, cut into small cubes

1 cup cilantro leaves

Sal de gusano or Chile Lime Salt (page 100)

1 avocado, halved, pitted, peeled, and diced

1 fresh red árbol or red serrano chile, thinly sliced for garnish

Cook the potatoes in boiling salted water until they are tender but still hold their shape. Drain and let cool, then thinly slice.

Meanwhile make the tostadas: fill a very large cast-iron skillet one-third full with olive oil and heat until a deep-fry or instant-read thermometer registers 350°F. Add the tortillas 2 or 3 at a time and fry until golden brown, about 2 minutes per side. Remove from the oil and drain on a rack set over a baking sheet or a large plate lined with paper towels. Set aside.

Make the vinaigrette: Combine the roasted garlic, lime juice, olive oil, honey, salt, pepper, and red onion in a small bowl and whisk to blend. Taste and add more salt if needed.

Combine the octopus, tomatoes, potatoes, radishes, cucumber, and cilantro in a medium bowl. Add the vinaigrette and mix well.

Arrange 2 tostadas on each plate. Place a large spoonful of the octopus mixture on each tostada and garnish with a sprinkle of sal de gusano or chile lime salt. Garnish with the diced avocado and chile. Serve immediately.

DISCOVERING PRAWNS

The first time we threw Maya prawns on the grill, it was as if none of us had really smelled a crustacean until that moment. The whole kitchen filled with the scent of fire and smoke and sea. They were a delicate pink, more like a seashell than that bubblegum color you usually get, and the flesh was so sweet it was as though they were brushed with a touch of honey. From that moment, we would buy shrimp whenever we could.

The shrimpers came in every three weeks or so. They worked a stretch of the Gulf Coast past Campeche called Laguna de Términos: End of the Lagoon. The interconnected lagoons and estuaries are protected by the government, so the only people you see are fishermen or the military. You can't send out a trawler in this water. Instead, you shrimp with hand–cast nets. You stand in the water and throw the net so that it fans out from you, then you let it settle and pull it in.

Once you realize what goes into getting these beautiful shrimp, you get obsessed. If the delivery truck breaks down, we'll send taxis packed with ice to go get the shrimp. It's a six–hour drive from Tulum. It's worth it.

Although it's hard to get super-fresh prawns or shrimp like the ones we use, get the biggest, freshest ones you can find. Try not to overcook them. Watch closely as they go from translucent to opaque, and touch them to make sure they're just firm. There's nothing sadder than rubbery shrimp.

The spicy beet greens are our Caribbean take on kimchi—and a delicious way to deal with the greens we end up with after roasting beets all day. Note that the spiced beet greens must be refrigerated overnight.

SERVES 6

MAYA PRAWNS with CHIPOTLE MEZCAL SAUCE

2 bunches beet greens, washed well

¼ cup sugar

1 tablespoon plus 2 teaspoons kosher salt

1 carrot, peeled and julienned

1 bunch scallions, cut into 1-inch lengths

2 tablespoons minced garlic

1 cup Chipotle Mezcal Sauce

2 pounds Maya prawns or extra-large head-on shrimp (U10 or U12), shells slit down the back but left on, veins removed

Olive oil

Freshly ground black pepper

1 tablespoon chile powder

1 cup thinly sliced cucumbers

½ cup thinly sliced radishes

3 mandarin oranges or clementines, suprêmed (see page 45)

Remove the stems from 1 bunch of beet greens. Put the greens in a bowl, sprinkle with 2 tablespoons of the sugar and 1 tablespoon of the salt, and massage into the greens. Let sit for about 30 minutes, or until wilted.

Drain the greens and place in a clean large bowl. Add the carrot, scallions, garlic, and ¾ cup of the chipotle mezcal sauce and mix well. Transfer to a nonreactive container, cover, and refrigerate overnight.

Prepare a grill for high heat. (Prawns should be cooked quickly, so you need to have the embers going.)

Put the prawns in a large bowl. Drizzle with olive oil, sprinkle with salt and pepper and the chile powder, and mix well. Oil the grill grate and grill the prawns until the flesh is just opaque and nice grill marks have formed, about 1 minute per side. Remove from the heat and let cool.

While the prawns cool, put the cucumbers in a small bowl and sprinkle with the remaining 2 tablespoons sugar and 2 teaspoons salt. Let sit for about 10 minutes.

Remove the stems from the second bunch of beet greens and put the greens in a large bowl. Add the wilted beet greens and mix well.

Divide the cucumber among six plates. Arrange the beet greens on top of the cucumber and scatter the radishes and mandarin oranges over them. Place the prawns on top and drizzle with the olive oil and the remaining ¼ cup of sauce.

CHIPOTLE MEZCAL SAUCE

MAKES ABOUT 2 CUPS

1 cup chipotle chiles in adobo sauce

2 tablespoons fresh lime juice

¼ cup white vinegar

¼ cup mezcal

⅓ cup water

1½ teaspoons kosher salt

Combine all the ingredients in a blender and blend on high until smooth, adding more water if needed.

The second you put a split lobster on the grill you're hit with that delicious smell of singeing shell, and all of your senses come alive. Maybe it's because we're conditioned to revere lobster: it's special-occasion food.

The lobsters we get in the Caribbean are beautiful—they don't have claws, and the tails are mild and sweet. You don't need to do much to the meat when it's this fresh and flavorful and grilled over flames. (Just don't overcook the lobster and make it chewy.) At Hartwood, we serve it with a simple pan sauce made with epazote; use it if you can find it, but if not, substitute tarragon or fennel fronds. And we always serve it with creamed yuca, our version of mashed potatoes. SERVES 2

GRILLED LOBSTER with CREAMED YUCA

One 1½- to 2-pound live lobster

¼ cup coconut or olive oil

Kosher salt

1 cup thinly sliced red onion (sliced lengthwise)

2 tablespoons mashed Roasted Garlic (page 62)

2 large dried guajillo chiles, toasted in a dry skillet until fragrant

4 tablespoons unsalted butter

1 cup heirloom cherry tomatoes

½ cup orange juice

¼ cup epazote leaves (or substitute tarragon leaves or fennel fronds)

Creamed Yuca (page 103)

¼ cup cilantro leaves

1 lime, halved, for garnish

Prepare a grill for medium heat, building your fire so that you have a balance of embers and flame.

Meanwhile, hold the lobster belly side down on a cutting board, with the head toward you. Plunge a cleaver or sharp chef's knife into the head and pull it toward you to cleave the head and kill the lobster instantly. Then split the lobster cleanly down the center with the cleaver so that it's completely severed into two halves. Rub the meat with the coconut oil and season with salt. Put the lobster shell side down on the cooler side of the grill—no direct fire for now—for 5 minutes.

Meanwhile, make the sauce: Place a 10-inch cast-iron skillet on the hottest part of the grill. Once it's nice and hot, sweat the onion, garlic, and chiles in the butter, until the onion softens. Add the tomatoes, season with salt, and add the orange juice. Simmer to reduce by half, then add the epazote. Move to a cooler part of the grill to keep warm.

Oil the grill grate, then flip the lobster meat side down over medium heat and grill for 4 minutes, pressing gently with a spatula to get some nice grill marks. Turn the lobster over and cook for 4 minutes. Move the skillet of sauce close to the lobster and place the lobster shell side down in the pan. Cook, basting the lobster continually with the sauce, for 5 minutes.

Spoon the yuca onto a platter, top with the lobster, and pour the sauce over everything. Garnish with the cilantro leaves and lime halves.

Every day when we'd drive past the bay on the way to work, we see guys out there netting sardines. And there were always pelicans swooping in and eating the catch, so we figured they must be delicious.

These are especially good with a cocktail. Maybe it's the chile lime salt—or the fact that they're fried. The sardines that we get have beautiful stripes on them. You can't find them in the States, but you will be happily surprised by how affordable—and good—fresh sardines are. SERVES 6

FRIED SARDINES with CHILE LIME SALT

1 pound fresh sardines

About 4 cups canola oil for deep-frying

1 cup all-purpose flour

1 teaspoon kosher salt

1 teaspoon freshly ground black pepper

1 teaspoon Chile Lime Salt (page 100)

An assortment of pickles (pages 54–59) for serving

Slice the sardines open along the belly and remove the intestines. Rinse the fish in cold water, drain, and pat dry with paper towels. To butterfly the sardines, cut each one open down the back from head to tail and gently spread them open.

Pour about 1½ inches of oil into a large deep skillet or pot and heat over medium-high heat until the oil reaches about 300°F. Meanwhile, mix the flour, salt, pepper, and chile lime salt in a baking pan until combined. Dredge the sardines in the flour mixture until coated, then remove, shake off any excess flour, and transfer to a plate.

Working in batches and being careful not to crowd the pan, add the sardines to the hot oil and cook for 3 minutes. Flip the fish and cook for another 3 minutes, or until golden brown and crispy. Remove to a paper towel–lined plate to drain. Serve immediately with pickles and, preferably, a cocktail.

You can serve these with any selection of pickles you want. At Hartwood, we use spring onions with habaneros (top), preserved nance with pickled white onions (center), and pickled nopales (bottom).

Preceding spread: Birds and fishermen line the shores in search of yellow-striped sardines. Delicious and always fresh, sardines are an everyman fish eaten often as a snack or as dinner.

We break down thirty whole fish a day, some as large as 80 pounds (this wahoo is about 38 pounds). We always use a thin, sharp knife and a clean cutting board. The first incision is along the collar, right beneath the gills, and then we work down the length of the back and into the flesh to cut the entire side from the spine. It takes practice to get it right. After you break down a dozen fish, you'll start to get the hang of it.

When you're served a fish fillet that is all white, it makes you feel like you're eating nothing special. It's better to have that almost burnt, crispy texture on the outside, going toward rare on the inside—treating fish like meat is the best way to think about it.

A fillet ends up dry when the cook isn't confident. It's overcooked to begin with, and then—once it's off the heat—he lets it sit in the hot skillet for another (lethal) 40 to 50 seconds. Here's how to avoid that: start the fish on the grill, skin side down (if the skin is still on) then place it in a skillet, grilled side up, and finish cooking it in the oven, allowing the two stages of cooking to meet in the middle. It's about one-quarter of the time on the grill, three-quarters in the oven, and it happens very quickly.

Coronado is a firm fish, so to check the doneness, feel the top and sides toward the end of the cooking time. You want the flesh to still give a little bit.

When you grill the pineapple, you want to really caramelize it to intensify the sweetness so that it carries through when combined with the chaya and oregano. Too little charring and sweetness, and it will all taste a little flat.   SERVES 4

GRILLED CORONADO FILLETS with PIÑA and CHAYA

1 pineapple

4 coronado or other lean, white-fleshed fish fillets (6 to 8 ounces each), skinned

½ cup sour cream

1 teaspoon ground dried árbol chile

¼ cup Roasted Chile Oil (page 63)

½ teaspoon mashed Roasted Garlic (page 62)

Kosher salt and freshly ground black pepper

½ white onion, thinly sliced

2 tablespoons unsalted butter

3 tablespoons olive oil

1 tablespoon honey

2 cups chaya (or spinach) leaves

¼ cup fresh oregano leaves

Juice of 1 lemon

Yes, that's a bee on the pineapple! There are plenty of bees in the kitchen, but they're never a concern. We have smokers that burn copal—a type of tree resin—to keep the bees in a calm state. Even in June, when it's very dry and flowers are not plentiful (and the bees can't resist the honey we cook with), no one gets stung.

Trim and peel the pineapple. (Core it now if you happen to have a pineapple corer; otherwise, proceed.) Cut the pineapple into ½-inch-thick rings. Use a sharp round cookie cutter to cut out the core from each slice. Set aside.

Prepare a grill for high heat. Preheat the oven to 400°F. Remove the fish from the refrigerator and let stand for a few minutes.

Combine the sour cream, árbol chile, 1 tablespoon of the chile oil, the roasted garlic, ½ teaspoon salt, and ¼ teaspoon pepper and mix well. Set aside.

Put the coronado fillets on a plate and drizzle with 1 tablespoon of the chile oil, turning gently to coat. Season with salt and pepper. Oil the grill grate, then place the fillets on the grill and cook for about a minute, until grill marks form. Remove to a plate. Reduce the grill temperature to medium.

Add the remaining 2 tablespoons chile oil, the onion, and butter to a large cast-iron skillet and melt the butter on the stovetop. Place the fillets in the skillet grilled side up, and put in the oven. Cook for 5 minutes, then baste with the butter and cook for another 5 minutes. Remove from oven, transfer a plate, and let rest for 1 minute.

Meanwhile, put the pineapple in a large bowl and drizzle with 2 tablespoons of the olive oil and the honey, turning to coat. Season with salt and pepper. Place the rounds on the oiled grill over medium heat and cook, without moving the slices, for about 3 minutes each side, until a fork can be easily inserted into the pineapple. Remove and let cool slightly, then cut each slice into quarters. Set aside.

Put the grilled pineapple, chaya, and oregano in a large bowl. Add the lemon juice, the remaining 1 tablespoon olive oil, and salt and pepper to taste; mix gently.

To serve, divide the pineapple salad among four plates and place a dollop of chile cream on top. Place the fillets on top of the cream and spoon the butter and onions onto the fillets.

SEASON YOUR GRILL

The recipes in this book assume that you will be grilling on a cleaned and seasoned grill grate. If you don't clean and season your grill before every use, it's time to get into the habit.

Clean your grill by scraping it with a metal brush so that there are no chunks of what you cooked last week or last year stuck to the grate, and then season it by rubbing the grilling surfaces with a shred of a rag dipped in canola or olive oil. This is basic culinary hygiene. For some inexplicable reason, some cooks let gunk build up because they think it adds flavor, and they only season a grill when a recipe tells them to do so. These people are wrong. If you work at a restaurant and you don't clean and season your grill, you will hear from the chef. Keep it up, and you'll be moved off that station.

So let's get this straight: Clean and season the grill before every use. Clean and season the grill if you're grilling different ingredients. Clean and season your grill and, if you have any doubts, clean and season it again. Now you're ready to begin.

HOW TO GRILL A WHOLE FISH

When a whole fish comes off the grill, it can be a magnificent sight: those marks on the skin, the charred tail, the steaming flesh at exactly the right level of doneness so that it transitions from medium-rare to perfectly cooked just as you spear it with a fork. So when the flesh sticks or it's raw at the bone, the disappointment is that much more intense. You know what you're missing.

At Hartwood, we grill thirty or so whole fish every day. They usually look pretty good. This is how we do it.

CONSIDER A BIGGER FISH. Choose a fish that feeds four instead of four fish that feed one each. A bigger fish will have slightly thicker skin that holds together, crisps up better, and won't stick to the grill as easily.

SCORE THE FLESH. After the fish has been cleaned and scaled, use a sharp knife to cut vertical incisions every 2 inches along the length of the body. Hold the knife so that it slices into the flesh at a 45-degree angle and slice all the way down to the bone. Repeat on the other side. The cuts help the fish cook more evenly, so that you avoid the problem of getting raw meat by the head and an overcooked tail.

GENEROUSLY OIL THE SKIN. Use plenty of oil, and make sure to cover the entire surface of the fish. A dirty grill is more likely to make the skin stick and the fish fall apart, but you don't need to be told again to clean and season the grill, because you're already in the habit of doing that.

FLIP THE FISH WHEN IT LETS YOU. Don't rush it. You want enough heat under the fish to crisp the skin while the flesh cooks.

The fish will tell you when it's ready. When you think it's time to flip the fish, use a spatula to gently raise it a tiny bit. If it lifts off the grill easily, it's time: the skin is cooked and it's no longer grabbing the grill grate. If it resists, wait and try again in 30 seconds.

Fresh fish from the sea to the oven: this red snapper was spear-caught about 100 meters from our kitchen.

Snapper is abundant in the Caribbean, and we always have it on the menu. We love its beautiful meatiness and its clean white flesh.

Dried avocado leaves have an anise-like flavor that can be approximated with fennel pollen or toasted ground fennel seeds, though it's more delicate. It's less a spice than an herb.   SERVES 4

RED SNAPPER with CHAYOTE and AVOCADO-LEAF DUST

1 cup dried split peas

4 cups water

Kosher salt

1 tablespoon unsalted butter

2 tablespoons heavy cream or crème fraîche

Salt and freshly ground black pepper

¼ cup ground dried avocado leaves or 3 pinches fennel pollen or ground toasted fennel seeds

¼ teaspoon ground cumin

½ teaspoon ground dried árbol chile

4 red snapper fillets (6 to 8 ounces each), skin on

3 tablespoons Roasted Chile Oil (page 63)

2 chayotes, peeled, pitted, cut into 1-inch-thick slices, then cut into thin strips

Olive oil

Place the split peas in a small saucepan, add the water, and season with salt. Bring to a boil, then lower the heat and simmer for 25 to 30 minutes, until the peas are tender. Drain, reserving about ½ cup of the cooking liquid.

Place the split peas in a blender. Add the butter, cream, salt and pepper to taste, half of the ground avocado leaves, the cumin, and chile and blend on high until thick and smooth, adding a little of the reserved cooking water if needed.

Meanwhile, prepare a grill for high heat. Preheat the oven to 350°F.

Put the fillets on a plate and drizzle with the chile oil, turning to coat thoroughly. Season with salt and pepper. Oil the grill grate, then add the fillets, skin side down, and cook for about 1 minute, or until nice grill marks have formed.

Transfer the fish to a large cast-iron skillet, skin side up, place in the oven, and cook for 15 minutes, until just cooked through and slightly browned at the thinnest edges.

Meanwhile, toss the chayote with olive oil to coat and season with salt and pepper. Place on the grill over high heat and cook until grill marks form, 30 seconds to 1 minute. Turn and repeat, then transfer to a cooler part of the grill to cook through, 2 to 3 minutes.

Just before serving, reheat the split pea puree.

Place a large spoonful of pea puree on each serving plate and arrange the grilled chayote alongside. Place the snapper fillets on the puree. Garnish with the remaining ground avocado leaves and serve.

GETTING GROUPER

At Hartwood, we always use wild-caught fish. There's a different taste to a fish that was caught and killed by hand: you can distinguish its true flavor on the plate, as opposed to it just tasting like . . . fish. And so all of the fish that we serve is caught by line—as in rod and reel—or spear.

Down here, you catch grouper by hunting. The fishermen will go four or five miles out to a reef. Some grouper are small, but when they spot a big grouper—say, 80 pounds—they'll slowly circle around, following it, seeing where it goes into its hole, what time it comes out in the morning, what time it goes back at night. Then they'll wait behind a rock, titanium spear in the gun (grouper will break any spear that's not titanium), hold enough breath to get underwater, take aim, and shoot. Hopefully they make a hit. That spear is connected to a line, and when the tip hits, the battle starts. Grouper are fast, aggressive, and big—they fight. Bull sharks that sense the blood will start circling in the shallows. (Sometimes a fisherman will also bring in a shark that we turn into empanadas or shark dip.)

Some days a grouper will come in that's 100 pounds. It takes two of us to carry it into the kitchen, where we need to break it down immediately so it will fit into the ice chests. We always cut around the part of the fish where the spear hit—the flesh there is traumatized and doesn't taste good. The rest of it? It's so magnificent, we serve the head and collar too.

THE HARTWOOD UNIFORM
It's too hot to cook in a chef's jacket, especially those poly-cotton blends supplied by the linen service companies, so the uniform here is a clean white T-shirt. If you get it dirty, douse it in bleach. You wear it until it gets an unprofessional-looking stain you can't get out, then you pull out a fresh one from the packages you keep stacked on the dresser. These aren't expensive T-shirts from some design atelier; they're Hanes crewnecks, two to a pack. A clean T-shirt and a pair of cutoffs, and you're dressed for work.

To know the sea like the land is one of the most difficult tasks and takes a lifetime to achieve. Felix (top and spearfishing for lobster at left) and Luis (bottom). We have been working with Luis—who is *el jefe*—and his son Martin for many years.

Grouper is a meaty, buttery fish, and when you roast it in the oven, all the juiciness comes through—it's like the steak of the sea. If you get a nice fat fillet, you can cook it a little longer and it won't dry out on you; it'll just get better, which is useful when you want to get extra-crispy skin. Grouper is forgiving.

The flesh is a surprisingly good match for beans. In this recipe, the white bean salad gets a little heat and smoke from roasted poblanos. It's tossed with the lime and honey vinaigrette we use in many of our salads, then topped with a cilantro crema. The fresh, herbal flavors of the cilantro are offset by the earthy sweetness of the roasted garlic we get when making roasted garlic oil. We use dried beans, which you will need to soak overnight. You can use 3 cups canned white beans if you want to take a shortcut, but dried beans taste better. SERVES 4

GROUPER with WHITE BEAN SALAD and CILANTRO CREMA

WHITE BEAN SALAD

1½ cups dried navy beans or other creamy white beans, soaked overnight in water to cover

1 onion, cut in half

1 carrot, peeled and cut in half

4 oregano stems

2 tablespoons kosher salt, or to taste

5 poblano peppers

Olive oil

4 cups arugula

½ cup cilantro leaves

½ cup Lime and Honey Vinaigrette (page 82)

4 grouper fillets (6 to 8 ounces each), skin on

Olive oil

Kosher salt and freshly ground black pepper

1 red onion, thinly sliced

8 tablespoons (1 stick) unsalted butter, cubed

CILANTRO CREMA

1 cup sour cream

¼ cup olive oil

1½ teaspoons mashed Roasted Garlic (page 62)

1 teaspoon kosher salt

1 teaspoon freshly ground black pepper

1 cup cilantro leaves (some tender stems are fine)

1 jalapeño, very thinly sliced

2 limes, halved

Preheat the oven to 400°F.

Prepare the beans and poblanos for the salad: Drain the beans and put in a large saucepan, along with the onion, carrot, and oregano. Add water to cover by 2 inches, then add the salt and boil gently over medium heat for 30 to 45 minutes, until the beans are soft. Drain the beans, discarding the onion, carrot, and oregano. Transfer to a bowl and let cool.

While the beans are cooking, coat the poblanos with olive oil, put on a small baking sheet, and roast for 20 minutes. Flip the peppers and roast for 20 minutes longer, or until charred all over. Let the peppers cool, then remove the seeds and skin. Cut into ½-inch-wide strips and fold into the white beans. Set aside.

Reduce the oven temperature to 350°F.

Coat the grouper fillets with olive oil and season with salt and pepper. Oil the grill grate and grill the fish skin side down for about 1 minute to get nice grill marks. Turn 45 degrees and cook for 1 minute longer. Flip and repeat.

Put the red onion and butter in a large cast-iron skillet. Transfer the fish, skin side up, to the skillet and drizzle olive oil over the skin. Roast in the oven until just cooked through, about 10 minutes.

Meanwhile, add the arugula and cilantro to the white beans and stir gently to combine, being careful not to mash the beans. Add the vinaigrette and stir to incorporate.

Make the crema: Combine the sour cream, olive oil, roasted garlic, salt, and pepper in a blender and puree until smooth, about 30 seconds. Add the cilantro in two or three batches, pulsing for about 10 seconds after each addition. Transfer to a bowl, cover, and refrigerate until ready to serve.

Spoon the salad onto individual plates and drizzle with the cilantro crema. Top with the grouper and red onions. There will be some brown butter left in the skillet—pour it over everything. Garnish with the jalapeño slices (about 2 per fillet) and limes.

At Hartwood, we apply the nose-to-tail philosophy to fish. When it comes to large fish like grouper, we use the cheeks, the collar, the head—even the marrow from the spine (delicious in ceviche). Most fish markets in the United States don't sell heads, but if you know your fishmonger, you can ask him to save some large ones for you. Grouper cheeks have a meaty consistency and almost a sweetness to them. Once you get the hang of cutting them, you'll wonder why anyone throws away the heads.

Depending on the size of the grouper, the cheeks can be as small as a cherry or as big as an orange. The cheek is a muscle that gets a lot of work, so it has a richer flavor and it holds its shape in the pan—you can sear it like a scallop.   SERVES 4

PAN-ROASTED GROUPER CHEEKS with RADISHES and TOMATOES

1 bunch radishes with greens

4 grouper heads

3 tablespoons olive oil

Kosher salt and freshly ground black pepper

2 tablespoons unsalted butter

Pickled White Onions (page 54), plus about ½ cup of the pickling liquid

4 small tomatoes, halved

¼ cup basil leaves

Pickled Nance (page 54), optional

2 limes, halved, for garnish

Preheat the oven to 350°F.

Put the radishes in a small baking pan, add 2 cups water, and cover the pan with aluminum foil. Roast for 45 minutes, or until the radishes are tender.

Meanwhile, remove the grouper cheeks: Starting right below the eye on one side of the head, insert the point of a paring knife into the skin at a 45-degree angle and twist it in a circle, letting the blade follow the bone. Stop just before you complete the circle, leaving a tab of skin to connect it, then place your knife parallel to the skin and use one smooth cut to detach the cheek from the skin. Be forceful but delicate. Repeat with the second cheek and then the remaining heads.

When the radishes are done, remove them from the oven and increase the temperature to 400°F. Drain the radishes and pat dry, then transfer to a small baking sheet. Toss with 1 tablespoon of the oil and season with salt and pepper. Roast for about 15 minutes, until the radishes begin to brown. Remove from the oven.

Meanwhile, cook the cheeks: Heat a large cast-iron skillet over high heat. Add the remaining 2 tablespoons oil and heat until shimmering. Sprinkle the grouper cheeks with salt and pepper and gently place in the pan. Once the cheeks are browned on the bottom and the meat has begun to give and become whiter on top, flip them over and add the butter to the pan. Once the butter has melted, reduce the heat, baste the cheeks, and sauté until cooked through, about 45 seconds. Remove from the heat.

Combine the onions, tomatoes, and basil in a bowl and toss with ½ cup of the pickling liquid. Taste and add a little more pickling liquid if desired.

To serve, place some roasted radishes on each plate and arrange the salad on top. Add 2 grouper cheeks to each plate and spoon the butter from the pan on top of them. Garnish with the pickled nance and limes.

Chances are you're not going to make this dish anytime soon. The grouper in your fish market probably weigh 5 to 10 pounds, while the grouper we get are usually between 80 and 120 pounds. But maybe your fish market will score a massive grouper, or you'll find yourself on a fishing trip with some experienced anglers, or you're an experienced angler yourself. It could be that you're on a road in Mexico and come across a fisherman with an 80-pound grouper in the back of his truck that he's willing to sell to you—in which case you'll know what to do, because you'll have committed this recipe to memory.

When you get a grouper that big, the collars can weigh as much as 8 pounds. Each of the two pieces is lined with long, concave bones that make the flesh a little more buttery and a little sweeter than the rest of the flesh—and relatively hard to eat. You need to work around the bones and pick at the meat, which is not what most restaurant-goers want to do. For the longest time, we would trim out the cheeks and put them on the menu, but the collar was for family meal—seasoned with salt and pepper, roasted in the oven, and served with a pile of tortillas and some cut-up limes. We'd all gather around the collars, pull off the meat, and eat the best fish tacos in Tulum.

Eventually, though, we wondered, what about the way Japanese chefs work with collars? We could roast the collar whole just as we already did, but if it was going to be served in the restaurant, we had to bring up the flavor: sal de gusano, honey, fresh chiles, and chile oil. The question was if people would understand it. The answer is, yes, they do. These days we go through about six grouper a week. Our regular customers snap up the collars. SERVES 4

ROASTED GROUPER COLLAR

A set of collars from 1 huge grouper
  (2 to 4 pounds each)

¼ cup Roasted Chile Oil (page 63)

Kosher salt and freshly ground
  black pepper

1 bunch spring onions or scallions

2 habaneros

VINAIGRETTE

2 tablespoons fresh lime juice

6 tablespoons olive oil

½ small shallot, minced

½ teaspoon mashed Roasted Garlic
  (page 62)

½ teaspoon honey

Kosher salt and freshly ground
  black pepper

SALAD

¼ cup thinly sliced radishes

¼ cup lime suprêmes (see page 45;
  optional)

½ cup beet greens, thoroughly washed

½ cup mizuna

¼ cup hoja santa leaves, cut into
  1–inch pieces (optional)

½ teaspoon sal de gusano or
  Chile Lime Salt (page 100)

Preheat the oven to 400°F.

Toss the grouper collars with 2 tablespoons of the chile oil and salt and pepper to taste in a roasting pan. Roast for about 25 minutes, until nicely browned.

Meanwhile, put the spring onions and habaneros on a small baking sheet and toss with the remaining 2 tablespoons chile oil and salt and pepper to taste. Roast until the onions and habaneros start to brown, 10 to 15 minutes.

Make the vinaigrette: Put the lime juice, olive oil, shallot, roasted garlic, and honey in a small bowl and whisk to combine. Add salt and pepper to taste. Set aside.

Make the salad: Combine the radish slices, lime suprêmes, if using, beet greens, mizuna, and hoja santa, if using, in a small bowl. Add ¼ cup of the vinaigrette and toss well. Taste and add more vinaigrette if needed.

Place the roasted spring onions and habaneros on a serving platter. Arrange the salad on top and set the roasted collars on the salad. Sprinkle with the sal de gusano or chile lime salt.

We make this soup for family meal. It's delicious enough to put on the menu, but it's not the kind of dish that would sell at Hartwood—people come here for pork ribs, grilled lobster, and grouper fillets, not for a soup made with fish heads. We build flavor by grilling the fish heads and vegetables, toasting the dried chiles, and adding the herbs we always have on hand, like chamomile, oregano, and avocado leaves. Those seemingly small steps make all the difference.

We use three types of dried beans for this dish, but you can use just two (1½ cups each) or even all red kidney or all lima beans. Soak them overnight.

SERVES 6 TO 8

FISH HEAD SOUP

2 medium fish heads or 1 large head (about 4 pounds total), gills removed, cleaned, scaled, and thoroughly rinsed

2 xcatic chiles (about 8 inches long), or poblanos or serranos

3 red or yellow bell peppers

8 tomatoes

1 white onion, quartered

1 red onion, quartered

8 cloves Roasted Garlic (page 62)

¼ cup Roasted Garlic Oil (page 62)

1 habanero, halved

5 dried árbol chiles, toasted in a dry skillet until fragrant

5 dried pequín chiles, toasted in a dry skillet until fragrant

3 cinnamon sticks

1 bunch chamomile or 1 cup dried chamomile or organic chamomile tea

½ cup dried oregano, preferably Mexican

2 dried avocado leaves or a pinch of fennel pollen (optional)

½ cup dried squash blossoms (optional)

1 tablespoon kosher salt, or to taste

1 tablespoon freshly ground black pepper, or to taste

6 quarts water

1 cup dried black beans, soaked overnight in water to cover

1 cup dried red kidney beans, soaked overnight in water to cover

1 cup dried lima beans, soaked overnight in water to cover

1 tablespoon honey

Diced avocado, chopped red onion, lime slices, cilantro leaves, and fresh tortillas for serving

Prepare a grill for high heat or preheat the oven to 450°F.

Oil the grill grate and cook the fish heads for about 5 minutes per side, until charred. Transfer to a large plate. Grill the chiles, peppers, tomatoes, and onions until good grill marks form. Alternatively, if you don't have a grill, put all the ingredients on a baking sheet and roast until nicely browned, 20 to 30 minutes.

Combine the fish heads, grilled vegetables and chiles, roasted garlic cloves and oil, habanero, dried chiles, cinnamon sticks, herbs, avocado leaves, and squash blossoms, if using, and salt and pepper in a large stockpot. Add the water and bring to a boil, then reduce to a simmer and cook for 1 hour.

Remove the fish heads and let cool. Strain the stock into another large pot and return to medium heat. Drain the soaked beans and add to the stock, along with the honey. Season the stock to taste and cook until the beans are tender, 45 minutes to 1 hour.

Meanwhile, pick the meat from the fish heads and reserve.

Taste the soup and season again if needed. Ladle the soup into bowls and add the fish. Serve with avocado, red onion, lime, cilantro, and tortillas.

La Tierra

THE LAND

It's great to go to a restaurant near the beach and eat fresh fish. So why do we go through twelve racks of pork ribs a night? Because we have some really good meat in the Yucatán. Who knew that the cool waters from the cenotes would bubble up on farms, making the perfect muddy home for slate-gray Yucatán pigs? Or that we'd be able to ask the guy who grows our chaya to breed rabbits, then have the local butcher grind the meat into spicy sausage according to our recipe? For the best grass-fed beef,

Preceding: All work on the milpas, which have some of the most beautiful red-soil farmland in the Yucatán Peninsula, is done by hand. Machines or trucks can't move the harvest over the region's narrow trails. Just from looking at the workers' hands you know who puts in the labor and carries the wisdom of years.

we have to look north to Monterey, so we don't serve it very often, but it's a worthy indulgence.

As much as we love creating ceviches and grilling whole fish, the play of sweet and spicy that is the basis of Hartwood's palate lends itself perfectly to meat crisped over wood and infused with smoky flavor.

All of these recipes can be served family-style. When you're on vacation, it's much more fun to share. Pull out your platters, invite your friends, and try it.

The DNA of the restaurant is in this recipe. The pork rib was on the menu when we opened (it has always been the most popular dish here, and during high season, we serve forty orders a night), but the idea behind the dish can be traced back to when we first started thinking about moving to Tulum. The technique is a mash-up of New York City and the Yucatán, of restaurant cooking and what you can do in the jungle, of savory and sweet.

Actually, it's pretty simple; you just need to invest the time. You braise the pork ribs overnight or first thing in the morning, reduce the cooking liquid, and then use that to baste the meat as you reheat the ribs: baste, wait, baste, wait, baste, wait, baste until the liquid becomes a glaze. There's no shortcut. Either you put in the time and it's delicious, or you don't and it's just fine.

Chances are you won't make the recipe quite the way we do. We use a banana leaf to cover the ribs and Cerveza Ceiba, from the Yucatán, for the braising liquid; you can use parchment paper instead and a medium-dark beer such as Negra Modelo. Whatever you do, don't compromise on the quality of the ribs—the pork in the Yucatán is gorgeous, all those happy pigs rooting around in the jungle mud. And try to find a dark honey, either at a farmers' market or a health food store. Its added depth will make a difference. There's nothing quite like the smell of pork and dark honey cooking together in the oven. SERVES 4

COSTILLAS

1 onion, roughly chopped

2 carrots, roughly chopped

2 celery stalks, roughly chopped

1 cup roughly chopped pineapple

3 pounds bone-in pork ribs

One 12-ounce bottle Cerveza Ceiba
or other medium-dark beer, such
as Negra Modelo

¾ cup dark honey

2 tablespoons star anise pods

2 tablespoons kosher salt, or more to taste

1 tablespoon freshly ground black pepper

1 banana leaf (optional)

Preheat the oven to 300°F.

Scatter the onion, carrot, celery, and pineapple over the bottom of a large baking pan. Place the ribs on top. Add the beer and honey then add enough water to reach halfway up the side of the ribs. Add the star anise, salt, and pepper. Lay the banana leaf or a sheet of parchment paper on top of the ribs, then cover the pan tightly with aluminum foil.

Cook the ribs for 7 hours, or until a knife easily pierces through the meat.

Remove the foil and banana leaf and put the pan back in the oven for 30 minutes, or until the ribs are nicely browned. Remove from the oven, transfer the ribs to a cutting board, and allow to cool enough to handle.

Meanwhile, strain the braising liquid into a saucepan and set over medium heat. Bring to a simmer and simmer until reduced by one-third. Remove from the heat and skim off the fat.

Portion the ribs for serving (make sure they're not too hot, or the meat will fall apart). Working in batches, place as many ribs as you can fit into a large cast-iron skillet, set over medium heat on the stove, and add 1½ cups of the braising liquid. Cook, basting the ribs every minute or so, until the liquid reduces to a caramel-like glaze, about 15 minutes. (If you would like more color, continue to cook, basting every 5 minutes, until the ribs are a darker caramel color.) Stop once the sauce is thick and coats the ribs. Season with salt to taste.

TWO SECRETS TO GRILLING MEAT

First, let it come to room temperature before cooking. That doesn't mean pulling it out of the refrigerator just before you put it on the grill; it means letting it sit, covered, for at least 30 minutes (for a smaller cut) and more than an hour (for a thick cut) so that the interior of the meat is close in temperature to the surface. It makes the cooking much more consistent.

Second, bring the same level of acuity to resting the meat as to cooking it. As a general rule, you rest grilled or pan-seared meat for half of the cooking time, turning it so that it rests on both sides. The flip is essential: if you don't turn it, the juices will drain and pool on the plate, and you want those juices in the meat.

If the total cooking time is 20 minutes, you want to rest the meat for 10 minutes—5 minutes on either side. Follow this formula for all the meat you grill—skirt steak, lamb, pork—and you'll notice the difference.

Sweet and spicy, tender, juicy, crispy: boneless pork belly after 7 hours in the oven. Recipe on next page.

One day Antonio, a mason who helped build Hartwood from the ground up (and some of whose ten children have worked in the restaurant), brought in some pure agave nectar—the real stuff from the succulent plant, preservative-free and unfiltered, with some flakes of leaves left in it. He began pouring it onto roasted habaneros and popping them into his mouth. It seemed it was going to be SO spicy. Imagine: a whole habanero in your mouth? You would need a week to get over that much heat. But he seemed fine. It turns out the agave provides an incredible balance to the hot pepper (though there's still a mild burn). And it works beautifully against the fat of the pork belly as a glaze.

You'll need to start the pork belly the day before you serve it. The long, slow cooking, plus weighting it down in the fridge overnight, makes it extra tender beneath its layer of grill-crisped fat. SERVES 6 TO 8

AGAVE PORK BELLY with GRILLED PIÑA

One 4-pound bone-in pork belly or 3½-pound boneless pork belly

4 teaspoons kosher salt

2 teaspoons freshly ground black pepper

6 poblano chiles, coarsely chopped

3 habaneros, sliced into ¼-inch-thick rounds, seeds removed

3 serrano chiles, chopped

1 cup agave nectar

2 cups water

1 large ripe pineapple (about 3½ pounds)

¼ cup best-quality apple cider vinegar

Preheat the oven to 250°F.

Season the pork belly all over with the salt and pepper. Put all the chiles in a large roasting pan and place the pork belly skin side down on top. Drizzle with ½ cup of the agave. Pour the remaining ½ cup agave and the water into the pan.

Cover the pan tightly with two layers of aluminum foil, transfer to the oven, and cook for 3 hours, carefully loosening the foil and basting the pork with the pan juices every hour.

Turn the pork over, cover, and cook until very tender, about 4 more hours.

Transfer the pork to another roasting pan; if it is bone-in, remove and discard the bones. Strain the cooking liquid into a saucepan (there should be about 5½ cups); reserve the chiles. Gently boil the juices until reduced and thickened to a glaze (about 1¼ cups liquid), 45 to 50 minutes. Add the reserved chiles and remove from the heat. Let cool, then refrigerate.

Meanwhile, cover the pork with a sheet of parchment or waxed paper or a small baking sheet. Top with a large plate and put weights, such as large cans, on top. Refrigerate overnight.

The next day, bring the pork belly to room temperature. Prepare a grill for medium-high heat.

Trim and peel the pineapple (if you have a pineapple corer, core the pineapple now). Cut the pineapple into ½-inch-thick rounds. Remove the core from each round with a small round cutter.

Brush the grill grate with oil. Grill the pineapple until nicely charred, 2 to 3 minutes per side; set aside. Let the grill cool to medium heat.

Reheat the glaze. Slice the pork belly into 1-inch-thick slices, arrange on the grill, and brush with some of the glaze. Grill until warmed and crisp, about 3 minutes per side. Brush the pork again with some of the glaze.

To serve, place 2 or 3 pineapple slices on each plate. Spoon some glaze over, top with the pork belly, and drizzle with the vinegar.

ANTONIO'S FARM

We've worked with the Maya from the beginning, but it was hard to see what their world was really like, because they're private, and because Tulum is a bubble. So it was a huge deal when Antonio invited us to see his *milpa*, the small farm he has in the jungle.

Antonio started at Hartwood when it was just a clearing. He helped build the restaurant, along with his five sons. He also has five daughters, and sometimes a few (or all) of them would bring us lunch and cold tamarind juice. When the restaurant opened, Antonio stayed on. He lives in Valladolid, which is about two hours from Tulum, and rather than go back and forth, he spends the work week in Tulum and his days off at home. On Mondays, though, he is alone on his farm, which is a short drive from Valladolid. He takes a taxi to an unmarked path on the side of the highway, then he heads out on foot. It takes him about forty-five minutes to reach his milpa.

To an American, it looks nothing like a farm. It looks abandoned. There are no tidy rows of black soil, just a lunar landscape of exposed rock and pockets of dirt with some green things growing randomly, a few fruit trees here and there. But if you stand still and look, you start to notice hundreds of butterflies—yellow, orangeish, and white. Get closer to those green things, and you realize they're squash vines, tomatoes, corn, beans, chiles, yuca, spiky pineapples, and sugarcane, and that the trees are heavy with papayas, mandarin oranges, mangoes, grapefruit, avocados, and Maya plums. There is order, but it's natural. Each plant is in just the right spot to take advantage of the sun, soil, and water tapped from the cenotes under the dry surface of the earth. What seems arbitrary at first is actually a farm that's in perfect harmony with its environment.

Antonio doesn't use fertilizer or pesticides. He doesn't need them, and besides, it would be too much work to carry the heavy bags and haul all that material from the side of the road. He built a *palapa*, an open-sided house with a thatched roof made of dried palm leaves, in the middle of the farm. There's a fire pit at one end, a place to hang up a couple of hammocks at the other. It's simple and rough. It's perfect.

When he's there, he'll harvest fruit and vegetables, or hunt for deer. There's another plot of land with maize, and one with beehives—we use his honey at Hartwood. Then he packs up everything in sacks he slings over his shoulder for the walk back to the road. Sometimes he heads out at night—without a flashlight. He lets the moon illuminate the limestone rocks on the path.

For us, the milpa is one of the most peaceful places on Earth. You find true silence there. It's also one of the most informative. It's one thing to follow the rhythms of a region by seeing what is available at the market, and another to understand those cadences by spending as much time as you can on the milpa and watching the plants grow, smelling the leaves, holding the fruit while it's still in the tree. In the restaurant, Antonio is the jack of all trades who does the hard work that keeps things running, but out here he's a teacher.

We wanted to thank Antonio by building a wood-burning oven on his farm, something big enough to feed all of his children and grandchildren. We asked around and hired Phoot Balam, a master oven builder who is more than eighty years old. He had hands like leather, could walk on uneven ground faster than most twenty-year-olds, and told dirty jokes all day long. It took him two months to finish the oven. It was built mostly with materials from the farm—rocks, dirt, hay.

The dome of the oven is a work of art. The vault was constructed from small, thin rocks that look like the scales on an armadillo. Phoot would finish one small part, let it set, and then finish another. Sometimes we would help and learn, but mostly he was out there by himself. It's intricate, but after curing in the sun, it's as solid as if it had been carved out of blocks. It's also enormous—the whole thing is the size of a small room, and the oven itself is large enough to handle two whole pigs. It looks like something that was built pre-man, an homage to the beginning of the world. It's a masterpiece. When you cook on it at night, the orange flames flicker in the door. Inside the oven it can be infernal, the powerful fire browning and blistering what you slide inside, but all you see is the dancing light. That's when you feel the magic of roasting with fire on the milpa.

LECHÓN

The first meal we cooked in Antonio's wood-burning oven was a *lechón*, baby pig. It's both simple and celebratory. The best way to cook lechón is at low heat for a long time—if you cover it, you can cook it and cook it and it won't dry out, it will just get more tender. Begin by cutting off the head and legs if necessary to get it to fit in your roasting pan (we used a hotel pan from the restaurant). Then roughly chop three or four white onions, one bunch of celery, and two or three scrubbed camotes (sweet potatoes) and put them in the roasting pan. Next you add your spices and chiles: allspice, cumin, a cinnamon stick, dried árbol chiles. Then you put the pig on top, drizzle it with a couple of tablespoons of olive oil and a half cup of honey, and season with salt and pepper. We cover it with a banana leaf, but you could use a sheet of parchment paper, pressing down so that it makes contact with the pig, and then cover tightly with two layers of aluminum foil.

If the heat is low, you can let the lechón go overnight, eight to ten hours. If it's higher, you might pull it out after three or four hours. There's no set time: it depends on the heat, and the size of the pig. The best way to tell if it's done is to take it out, uncover a corner of the pan, and poke at an edge of the meat with a fork. You know how you want it to flake apart, so either take it out or cover it again and put back in for a while longer.

When the lechón is ready, take it out of the pan and strain the liquid. Skim the fat off the top, but don't be too obsessive about it. Then reduce the liquid by half to concentrate the flavor.

When you're ready to eat, bring up the heat in the oven and put the pig back in the pan to heat the meat through and crisp up the skin. You can serve it on a platter, or cleave it into pieces and put it on plates. You can pour the reduced roasting liquid over it, or put it in a bowl to the side. You might make a few chile sauces, or just have a bowl of limes. You should make fresh tortillas and have a bowl of black beans. You could make the Jicama Salad (page 74), or the Blistered Plátanos (page 99), or the Toasted-Coconut Cake (page 227), but only if you feel like it. A whole lechón out of a wood-burning oven with a case or two of Negra Modelo is a party on its own.

The fact is, there are easier ways to feed yourself and
your friends. That's true of many of the recipes in this
book. You spend hours cooking in the middle of the
jungle—or in your backyard—because it connects
you to what you love.

This is a play on the classic Italian pairing of prosciutto and melon. It came about when we found the *melon de milpa*, which looks like a squash on the outside, but is pure melon inside. It ripens really fast, and when we have it at Hartwood, the kitchen smells intensely of fruit. As for the ham, it's impossible for us to cure here in this humid air. Instead, a nice, slow-grilled pork belly will get good and smoky.   SERVES 4

SLOW-GRILLED PORK BELLY with CACAO BEANS and MELON de MILPA

GLAZE

⅔ cup honey

¼ cup Roasted Chile Oil (page 63)

1 tablespoon mashed Roasted Garlic (page 62)

2½ teaspoons kosher salt

1 teaspoon freshly ground black pepper

3 tablespoons water

2 dried pasilla chiles

One 1¾-pound boneless pork belly, excess fat trimmed off

2 tablespoons cacao nibs

2 tablespoons *chapulines* (dried grasshoppers; optional)

1 melon de milpa or cantaloupe, halved, seeded, and sliced ½ inch thick

Make the glaze: Combine the honey, oil, garlic, salt, pepper, and water in a small saucepan and bring to a simmer. Add the chiles and cook until soft, about 8 minutes. Remove from the heat and let cool slightly, then puree in a blender until smooth.

Put the pork belly in a large bowl and rub with half of the glaze. Let marinate at room temperature for 1 hour.

Toast the cacao nibs and chapulines, if using, in a small dry cast-iron skillet for 2 minutes. Coarsely grind in a spice grinder and reserve for garnish.

Prepare a grill for high heat.

Oil the grill grate. Grill the pork belly over the hottest part of the grill for 2 minutes on each side to mark it, then grill over a medium-hot fire for 20 to 25 minutes, flipping the belly and brushing it with some of the remaining glaze every 10 minutes, until a knife easily pierces the thickest part. Transfer to a cutting board and let rest for 10 minutes.

Bring the remaining glaze to a boil in a small saucepan over high heat, then reduce the heat to low and cook for about 2 minutes, until slightly thickened.

Pour the glaze over the pork belly, then slice it and place on a serving platter. Sprinkle the ground cacao nibs and chapulines, if using, over the pork belly and serve with the melon alongside.

The pork chops in the Yucatán aren't the thick double-cut chops you get in the United States. They're thin, so they can be cooked quickly—a few minutes on the grill, a few more minutes resting off the heat, and you're done. We serve these with pickled eggs on the side because in this part of Mexico, it seems like there's always an egg on the side, or on top, or mixed into the sauce—a little bit of added nutrition that's characteristic of the food around here.

The porridge is made from amaranth grains, which were a staple of Aztec cooking. The grains are packed with nutrients—just like quinoa. Amaranth porridge made with milk will give you the same rich mouthfeel as creamy grits, and the pickled egg will wake up your palate.   SERVES 4

PORK CHOPS with AMARANTH PORRIDGE and GRILLED LEEKS

2 cups amaranth seeds

2 cups milk

Kosher salt

2 tablespoons unsalted butter

2 leeks, trimmed, halved lengthwise, washed, and dried

2 tablespoons Roasted Chile Oil (page 63)

Freshly ground black pepper

Four 4-ounce pork chops

2 Pickled Jamaica Eggs (page 59), halved

Prepare a grill for high heat. Oil the grill grate.

Combine the amaranth and milk in a large saucepan, add a pinch of salt, and bring to a simmer. Simmer for 10 to 20 minutes, or until tender. Stir in the butter. Taste and adjust the seasoning. Remove from the heat; reheat gently before serving.

Coat the leeks with some of the chile oil and season with salt and pepper. Grill until lightly charred, 5 to 10 minutes on each side. Let cool, then pull off the carbonized outer layer, being sure to keep some of the blackened parts.

Lightly coat the pork chops with the remaining chile oil and season with salt and pepper. Grill the chops until grill marks form, about 4 minutes, then turn and cook for another 4 minutes. Remove to a platter and let rest for 4 minutes, turning once.

Serve with the pickled eggs.

This recipe is for an enormous rib eye, a special occasion cut. The total cooking time is 20 minutes, so you want to rest it for 10 minutes—5 minutes on either side. Follow this formula for all the meat you grill (skirt steak, lamb, pork), and you'll notice the difference.   SERVES 4

RIB EYE with PEPITA-LIME BUTTER

One 28-ounce bone-in rib eye

1 tablespoon allspice berries, toasted in a dry skillet until fragrant and ground

Kosher salt and freshly ground black pepper

12 fresh árbol chiles (or substitute 4 serranos or jalapeños)

2 habaneros

PEPITA-LIME BUTTER

4 tablespoons unsalted butter, softened

1 teaspoon pepitas (pumpkin seeds), toasted in a dry skillet until fragrant, then ground

1 tablespoon grated lime zest

1 lime, halved

Prepare a grill for high heat. Preheat the oven to 450°F.

Oil the grill grate. Season the rib eye with the allspice and salt and pepper. Cook the meat until grill marks form, about 2½ minutes, then turn it 45 degrees, to form a crosshatch pattern, and cook for another 2½ minutes or so. Repeat on the other side.

Transfer the meat to a large cast-iron skillet, put it in the oven, and cook for 10 minutes, basting the meat with its juices every 2 minutes. Remove to a cutting board and let it rest for 10 minutes, turning once.

Meanwhile, clean and oil the grill grate. Cook the fresh árbol chiles and habaneros until lightly charred, about 3 minutes per side. Transfer to a plate and season with a pinch of salt.

Make the pepita-lime butter: Combine the butter, pepitas, and lime zest in a small bowl and mix until smooth.

Slice the meat. Serve each portion topped with 1 tablespoon of the butter and garnish with the lime and the grilled chiles.

This a classic European preparation enlivened with ingredients from the Yucatán. First you braise the meat with aromatic vegetables, dried chiles (which give smoky heat), fresh chiles (which give fruity heat), and an avocado leaf (which has a faint taste of licorice). If you don't have access to an avocado tree, you can use fennel pollen or seeds to get some of the same flavor, but try to make this with the real thing if you can. Then you sear the short ribs to give them a brown crust, reduce the braising liquid into a sauce, and serve both over roasted corn that's pureed with chiles, lime, coconut water, and sour cream—it's creamed corn with a kick.

At Hartwood, the dish is meant for sharing. We have the butcher cut the short ribs into pieces that weigh up to 2 pounds and look like something Fred Flintstone would eat. However, these can be unwieldy in a home kitchen—you'd need a large pan for braising and a 12-inch cast-iron skillet for searing. The solution? Use shorter pieces—the flavor will be the same. If you want the full-sized ribs, you may need to order them ahead.

You can braise the short ribs earlier in the day and set them aside for an hour or so, until you're ready to serve, or cook them up to 3 days ahead and keep tightly covered in the refrigerator. SERVES 6

AVOCADO-LEAF SHORT RIBS with SERRANO-CHILE CREAMED CORN

SHORT RIBS

Three 1½- to 2-pound short ribs or six ¾- to 1-pound ribs

Kosher salt and freshly ground black pepper

3 yellow onions, roughly chopped

6 garlic cloves, crushed and peeled

6 carrots, peeled and cut into ½-inch-thick slices

3 red bell peppers, cut into ½-inch-thick slices

1 habanero chile, halved

6 dried ancho chiles, toasted in a dry skillet until fragrant

6 allspice berries

1 fresh avocado leaf (or a pinch of fennel pollen or 1 teaspoon fennel seeds)

CREAMED CORN

4 ears corn, husked

1 teaspoon Chile Lime Salt (page 100)

2 teaspoons unsalted butter

Juice of 1 lime

1 jalapeño

¾ cup sour cream

1 to 4 tablespoons coconut water

2 serrano chiles, roughly chopped

A knob of unsalted butter (optional)

Queso cotija for garnish (optional)

Pickled White Onions (page 54) for garnish (optional)

Preheat the oven to 350°F.

Season the short ribs with salt and pepper. Put the short ribs in a heavy braising pan or Dutch oven, add the remaining ingredients, and cover with water. Bring to a low boil on the stovetop, then transfer to the oven and braise for 1¼ hours, or until the meat is tender (it won't be pull-apart tender at this point, but it should be easily pierced with a knife). Remove the pan from the oven and cool to room temperature—the braise will continue to cook and the flavors will develop more.

While the short ribs are cooking, make the corn: Prepare a grill for high heat.

Season the corn with the chile lime salt, then wrap in a foil packet with the butter and lime juice. Grill until the corn is charred in spots. (Alternatively, grill the corn, without the foil, directly over a gas burner set to medium heat; melt the butter with the lime juice; reserve). Char the jalapeño on the grill or over a gas burner. Let the corn and jalapeño cool.

Carefully unwrap the corn, reserving the juices, and cut the kernels off the ears. Transfer to a blender, add the reserved juices (or the butter mixture), jalapeño, sour cream, and 1 tablespoon coconut water, and puree until smooth and thick, adding more coconut water if necessary. Add the serranos and blend well. Transfer to a saucepan. (The short ribs are served with an intense reduction sauce, so the corn is purposely underseasoned to balance the flavor. It will seem really spicy at this point, but don't worry.)

When you're ready to serve the dish, heat a large cast-iron skillet over medium-high heat. Remove the short ribs from the braising liquid, scraping any stray vegetables and chiles back into the pan. Strain the braising liquid and reserve the chiles; set the liquid aside. Add the short ribs to the hot pan and sear on all sides until brown, crisp, and heated through—the fat on the meat should do the trick, but if necessary, toss a knob of butter into the pan. (If the bones fall off, don't worry about it—you can reassemble the short ribs when you serve the dish.) When the short ribs are browned, pile them on a plate set close to the stove to keep them warm.

Lower the heat under the pan to medium, add the strained braising liquid and reserved chiles, and boil to reduce the liquid by two-thirds. Taste and adjust the salt and pepper as needed.

While the sauce is reducing, gently reheat the creamed corn.

To serve, spread a generous swoosh of creamed corn on each plate and put the short ribs on top. Spoon the sauce over, crumble some queso cotija on top if desired, and garnish with the pickled onions, if using.

We get veal only three or so times a year, and because the supply is limited, it's on the menu for just four or five days at a stretch. The meat is so creamy and delicate, you don't want to do too much to it. We season it with salt and allspice, which is one of the most important ingredients at Hartwood. Called *pimiento de Tabasco* in the markets, the allspice berries we get are a little more peppercorn-like than what you find in the United States.

Our pomegranates come from Campeche, where the trees grow wild. The seeds give a fruity burst to the dish.

The salsa recipe makes more than you will need for this dish. It keeps in the refrigerator for up to a week and is good with any grilled meat, especially steak.

SERVES 6

VEAL CHOPS with RED PEPPER-POMEGRANATE SALSA

Six 12-ounce veal rib chops

¼ cup Roasted Onion Oil (page 64)

¼ teaspoon allspice berries, toasted in a
   dry pan until fragrant and ground

Kosher salt

2 teaspoons freshly ground black pepper

Red Pepper–Pomegranate Salsa
   for serving

Baby greens, chick pea sprouts, and
   slivered chayote for garnish

Bee pollen for garnish (optional)

Prepare a grill for medium-high heat.

Put the veal chops in a bowl, drizzle with the roasted onion oil, and season with the allspice and salt to taste.

Oil the grill grate. Grill the veal chops for 4 to 5 minutes per side—the grill marks should be clear and the meat should feel firm. Let rest for about 2 minutes per side.

Smear some of the salsa over each plate and top with the chops.

Top with the greens. Sprinkle with the bee pollen, if using. Garnish with strips of chayote.

RED PEPPER-POMEGRANATE SALSA

MAKES 3 CUPS

1 red pepper

2 cups pomegranate seeds

¼ cup sugar

½ teaspoon salt

1 cup white vinegar

1 cup water

Pinch of habanero powder

Roast the red pepper to remove skin and seeds and set aside.

Combine the pomegranate seeds, sugar, salt, vinegar, water, and habanero powder in a medium saucepan and bring to a simmer over medium-high heat. Reduce the heat to medium-low and cook until reduced by two-thirds. Remove from the heat and let cool.

Put the red pepper and pomegranate seed mixture in a blender and blend on high until smooth, 30 to 45 seconds. Strain through a fine mesh sieve. Serve or store in refrigerator.

This dish changes depending on the chiles available in the market. We like it with poblanos, but you can use any chile that has an earthy flavor and medium heat. The chicken is first braised in a covered pan, which makes it juicy and succulent, then transferred to a cast-iron pan and crisped up in the hottest part of our wood-burning oven. (At home, you can either crank your oven as high as it will go or use the broiler—be sure to move the chicken around to expose as much of the skin to the flame as possible.) The braising liquid is reduced to concentrate the flavors of the chiles and tomatillos. Even after all of that, it's a surprisingly subtle dish.   SERVES 6

ROAST CHICKEN with POBLANOS and TOMATILLOS

One 4-pound chicken, excess fat trimmed

Kosher salt and freshly ground
  black pepper

1 head garlic (optional)

2 cups chicken stock or water

2 onions, roughly chopped

1 shallot, roughly chopped

4 garlic cloves, crushed and peeled

6 carrots, peeled and roughly chopped

3 celery stalks, roughly chopped

2 tomatillos, husked, rinsed, and quartered

2 poblano chiles, sliced

6 dried árbol chiles

Preheat the oven to 350°F.

Season the chicken with salt and pepper. If you have a head of garlic on hand, slice off the top and place in the cavity of the chicken—it's not necessary, but it adds flavor. Put the chicken in a cast-iron pan (with parchment and foil, if needed) or a Dutch oven and pour in the stock. Scatter the onions, shallot, garlic, carrots, celery, tomatillos, and chiles around the chicken.

Bring the stock to a low boil on the stovetop, then cover the pan, transfer to the oven, and braise for 30 to 45 minutes, or until the chicken is cooked through—the drumstick should move easily when wiggled.

Preheat the broiler (or, if the chicken won't fit below the heating element, preheat the oven to 500°F). Using tongs, transfer the chicken to a large cast-iron skillet; set the braising pan aside. Broil (or roast) the chicken, checking every couple of minutes, until the skin turns golden brown and crisp—move the pan around so that the chicken browns evenly. Transfer the chicken to a serving platter; reserve the skillet.

Strain the braising liquid and pour into the skillet. Bring to a simmer over medium heat, scraping up any browned bits in the bottom of the pan, and simmer until reduced by half. Taste and adjust the seasoning. Pour the liquid over the chicken and serve.

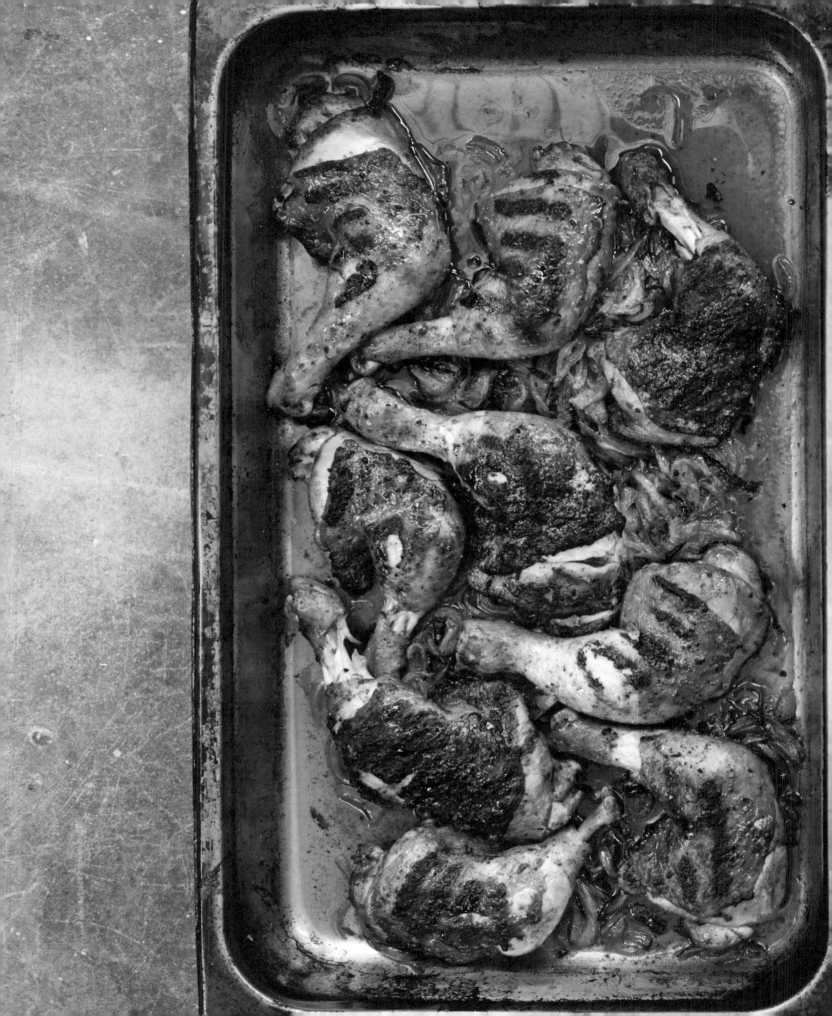

This is one of the standards of the Yucatán, Maya comfort food. First you make the *recado rojo* paste out of flavorful spices, then you dissolve that paste in a little bit of orange juice to use as a braising liquid for the chicken and to serve as a thin, brothy sauce. The key ingredient is achiote seeds (also called annatto seeds), which give the paste an amazing garnet color and add a peppery, nutmeggy flavor that pulls off the trick of tasting zingy and earthy at the same time.

You could pick up a block of recado rojo at a Mexican market, but this version tastes brighter than what you can buy in a package—the combination of cloves, cumin, and garlic is almost floral. The recipe yields more paste than you will need: store the extra in the refrigerator, where it will keep for 2 weeks, or give it away to friends.   SERVES 8

CHICKEN LEGS RECADO ROJO

RECADO ROJO

3 tablespoons achiote seeds

¾ cup orange juice

3 tablespoons coriander seeds

3 tablespoons cumin seeds

3 tablespoons cloves

3 tablespoons allspice berries

3 tablespoons black peppercorns

3 dried avocado leaves, shredded (or substitute 3 tablespoons fennel seeds)

3 tablespoons ground cinnamon

3 tablespoons dried oregano, preferably Mexican

6 large garlic cloves

1 tablespoon kosher salt

8 whole chicken legs

1 tablespoons kosher salt

2 tablespoons freshly ground black pepper

2 cups water

2 tablespoons apple cider vinegar

1 lime, halved, for garnish

Make the recado rojo: Soak the achiote seeds in the orange juice in a small bowl until softened, about 15 minutes.

Meanwhile, toast the coriander, cumin, cloves, allspice, and black peppercorns (plus the fennel seeds, if using) in a cast-iron skillet over medium heat until fragrant, 2 to 4 minutes. Let cool, then pulse in a spice grinder until finely ground. Mix with the cinnamon and set aside.

Pulse the oregano and avocado leaves in the spice grinder until fine, then sift through a fine-mesh sieve (to catch any fibers that weren't chopped up by the grinder) and set aside. Crush the garlic with the salt in a mortar and pestle until a rough paste forms.

Combine the achiote seeds with the orange juice, the spices, and garlic paste in a blender and blend until smooth, about 1 minute. Divide the paste into three ¼-cup portions. Wrap 2 portions and refrigerate for up to 2 weeks.

Prepare a grill for medium-high heat. Preheat the oven to 400°F.

Season the chicken legs with the salt and pepper. Oil the grill grate. Grill the chicken skin side down until the skin colors and clear grill marks form, about 8 minutes. Do not flip—you just want color on one side. Remove from the grill.

Dissolve the remaining ¼ cup recado rojo paste in the water and add the vinegar. Place the chicken legs grill marks up in a shallow baking pan. Pour the vinegar mixture into the pan and cover tightly with aluminum foil.

Put the chicken in the oven and cook for 45 minutes, or until cooked through. Uncover and return to the oven for 10 to 15 minutes to let the skin crisp up.

Serve with the braising liquid and lime. We might add some grilled onion, but no pressure!

MASA & TORTILLAS

Masa is one of those simple preparations that takes a lifetime to perfect. Basically, masa is the corn mash that becomes the base for tortilla dough. It's one of the foundations of civilization in this part of the world, the staple that fed the Mayas and that still feeds the Mexicans, and while everybody here eats tortillas, most buy fresh tortillas either directly from a *tortilleria* or from one of the coolers that the tortillerias stock in the markets and label with their names (the coolers keep the tortillas hot and steamy).

Those who make tortillas at home might use Maseca, a corn flour sold in any market that is mixed with water to make masa. Some might buy fresh masa from one of the street vendors you see standing on the sidewalk next to large plastic buckets filled with the corn mash. Few go through the trouble of making masa from scratch. It takes several days, and you need to put some sweat into it (not to mention the special equipment and ingredients). Buying masa from a vendor is much easier.

We go to the trouble because we think it's worth it. A tortilla made with fresh masa is like tasting a ripe tomato still warm from the vine. When it is cooked, the tortilla turns golden brown from the sugars, and it smells like toasted corn. It's a flavor so perfect and fleeting that it's hard to go back even to fresh tortillas from a tortilleria.

To make 4 pounds of masa, you will need:

1 tablespoon calcium hydroxide

1 cleaned metal bucket

2¼ pounds dried corn

1 lime, just in case

1 clamp-on hand grinder or a grinder attachment for a stand mixer

1 tortilla press

1 quart-size Ziploc bag, split into 2 pieces

Place the calcium in the bucket and add the dried corn and three times the amount of water by volume. Bring the water to a rolling boil (you can use a stockpot, but the bucket won't hold heat as well and will cool off fast, which is what you want) and boil for 30 to 45 minutes. You want to cook the corn until

it's just al dente: the skin will come off easily and the kernels should turn to white. If you overcook it, all is lost—this can happen in a matter of seconds and is the part that takes years to get right. So check the corn again and again. Pull out a kernel, take a bite, toss it back; repeat.

When the corn is ready, take the bucket off the heat and let it sit uncovered overnight at room temperature. (If using a stockpot, transfer the contents to another container to bring down the temperature.)

In the morning, rinse the corn 3 to 4 times in a sieve until the water runs clear and most of the flavor of the calcium hydroxide is gone. (If after rinsing you find that the corn tastes like zinc, it means you added too much calcium hydroxide. Make a note to use less next time. You can correct it by adding some lime juice, but you want to get to the point where you don't need to make that adjustment.)

Now place the rinsed corn in the hopper of a manual plate–style grinder and set the plate to the finest setting. Run the corn through until it comes out smooth. And there you have it: masa!

When you're ready to start making tortillas, heat a dry plancha or cast-iron pan over medium-high heat. Have a tortilla warmer lined with a napkin or dish towel ready. Pull off a piece of masa the size of a walnut (in the shell), hold it in the palm of one hand, and then use the thumb of your other hand to flatten it into a thick disk. If you've been doing this your entire life, you can make a tortilla with your bare hands, but the rest of us need to use a tortilla press lined with the two halves of the Ziploc to keep the dough from sticking. Place the piece of masa between the pieces of plastic, close the press, and push down firmly with the handle once or twice until the tortilla is thin. Carefully peel away the plastic, place the tortilla on the plancha, and cook until the edges began to curl up slightly and the bottom is nicely browned in spots, 30 seconds to 1 minute, depending on the heat, then flip and cook for another 15 seconds. Eat the first tortilla yourself, then make the rest. Put each finished tortilla in the warmer as you go, wrap the napkin around it, and cover the warmer; the steam helps soften the tortillas as they sit. You should have enough masa for about 6 dozen 4–inch tortillas.

Antonio's wife makes fresh tortillas with every meal. The smell of the masa on the fire is like no other.

The chile pequín gives off a really nice heat for such a small pepper. It's not as long-lasting as some chiles, so it's not going to build and carry through a whole dish. Instead, it wakes you up a little and adds to the flavor of the lamb in this recipe rather than overpower it. The chile pequín is used here in a dry rub because the lamb doesn't need much else.

We serve it with our grilled tomatillo and mint sauce for our version of the classic combination of lamb with mint. The sauce is a puree of distinctly Mexican ingredients—tomatillos, cilantro, toasted pepitas, and honey— but the mint comes through. And it's super-simple to make. You don't always have to work hard to get a lot of flavor.

A note on the lamb: we use lamb racks with the fat left on because we love how its surface absorbs the flavors of the chile, and because it crisps up nicely on the grill. When you trim the meat—i.e., if you "French" the rack— you lose so much of that fatty, gamy flavor. But if you prefer to trim it off, the recipe will still work.

This dish is also good with Pickled Spring Onions (page 54).   SERVES 6

CHILE PEQUÍN LAMB with TOMATILLO-MINT SAUCE

2 tablespoons pequín chiles

3 avocado leaves (or 1 tablespoon fennel seeds)

1 tablespoon allspice berries

2 racks of lamb (not Frenched)

Kosher salt and freshly ground black pepper

TOMATILLO-MINT SAUCE

4 tomatillos

¾ cup pepitas (pumpkin seeds), toasted in a dry skillet until fragrant

¼ Burnt Onion (page 64)

1 garlic clove, thinly sliced

1½ habaneros

1 cup mint leaves

½ cup basil leaves

½ cup cilantro leaves

¼ cup Roasted Garlic Oil (page 62)

Juice of 1 lime

1 tablespoon honey

1 teaspoon kosher salt

1 to 2 tablespoons coconut water or water (optional)

Freshly made corn tortillas, homemade (page 210) or store-bought for serving (optional)

Toast the chiles, avocado leaves (or fennel seeds), and allspice in a cast-iron skillet over low heat until fragrant, 1 to 4 minutes. Let cool, then pulse until fine in a spice grinder.

Sprinkle the spices over the lamb, pressing into meat and fat. Season with salt and pepper.

Prepare a grill for high heat.

Oil the grill grate. After the fire catches but before it settles into hot embers, quickly grill the tomatillos for the sauce. Set aside.

Grill the lamb over high heat for 5 minutes, turning once. Transfer to a medium-low area of the fire and cook for 10 minutes, turning once. Transfer the lamb to a cutting board and let rest for 5 minutes, turning once.

While the lamb is resting, finish the sauce: Put the pepitas in a blender and pulse until coarsely ground. Add the grilled tomatillos and the remaining ingredients (except the optional coconut water) and puree until smooth, about 1 minute. (If necessary, add coconut water.) Taste and adjust the seasoning.

Slice the racks into chops and serve with the sauce and, if desired, corn tortillas.

Los Dulces

DESSERTS

Some of the desserts at Hartwood ride the line between sweet and spicy, others are rustic and sweetened with honey. These flavors are subtle, which isn't to say that the desserts are delicate. The careful pastry techniques you might learn working in other restaurants aren't useful when you're mixing cake batters in this ever-changing humid air, then baking them in a wood-burning oven.

The recipes we use at Hartwood are more like guidelines than carefully measured formulas, as what we do is more a form of roasting than traditional baking. We developed forgiving recipes that can be adjusted when we sense that the barometric pressure is rising, or when we see that the wood is burning differently. If the top of the cake is burned to a solid black, we'll slice it off and mix up a honey-caramel glaze to pour over the top. The point isn't to execute a flawless pastry (impossible in this environment) as much as to make something tasty to wrap up the meal.

We have adapted the recipes in this chapter for a conventional oven, but if you ever have the chance, you should try to make one in a wood-burning oven. It might come out lopsided or charred, but the wood smoke imparts a flavor that can't be replicated in an oven you turn on with a knob.

People in the States might be into homemade nut milks, but the Mexicans figured out the most refreshing alt-dairy drink of all time: horchata. A mixture of toasted rice and warm spices that is soaked overnight in water, blended, and strained, it is incredibly refreshing and flavorful served over ice. These days most people make it from a mix, but the real thing is so easy and so good.

This cake plays on horchata's creamy deliciousness. If you make the whole recipe of horchata, you'll have a lot left over. Consider it a gift: drink an ice-cold glass (or two) of it while you make the cake.

Note that you'll need to start the horchata the night before.   SERVES 8

HORCHATA CAKE

CAKE

6 tablespoons sunflower oil

3 cups all-purpose flour

1 teaspoon baking soda

1 teaspoon kosher salt

1 teaspoon ground cinnamon

2 cups sugar

8 tablespoons (1 stick) unsalted butter, softened

3 large eggs

2 large egg yolks

½ cup plain whole-milk yogurt

½ cup Horchata (page 276)

2 teaspoons vanilla extract

FROSTING

12 ounces (1½ large packages) cream cheese, softened

¾ cup confectioners' sugar

2 tablespoons whole milk, or as needed

2 teaspoons light honey

½ teaspoon vanilla extract

¼ teaspoon kosher salt

Prickly pear syrup for garnish (optional)

Make the cake: Preheat the oven to 325°F. Grease a 10-inch springform pan with 1 tablespoon of the sunflower oil (you can line the pan with greased parchment paper if it is old and prone to sticking); set aside.

Whisk the flour, baking soda, salt, and cinnamon together in a medium bowl; set aside.

Using a handheld electric mixer on medium-high speed, cream the sugar, butter, and the remaining 5 tablespoons oil in a large bowl until light and fluffy (the mixture will resemble wet sand). Reduce the speed to medium-low and add the eggs one at a time, followed by the egg yolks, beating well after each addition. Add the yogurt, horchata, and vanilla, beating to blend. Slowly add the flour mixture, beating just to blend.

Pour the cake batter into the pan and lightly tap the pan against your work surface to eliminate any air pockets. Bake the cake for 1 to 1¼ hours, until a toothpick or tester inserted into the center comes out clean; the cake should pull away from the sides of the pan and be golden brown. Let cool completely.

Make the frosting: With a handheld mixer, blend the cream cheese, confectioners' sugar, milk, honey, vanilla, and salt together in a large bowl until smooth and creamy; if necessary, add another splash of milk.

Remove the sides of the pan and slide the cake onto a serving plate. Frost the sides of the cake, then frost the top generously with the remaining frosting, using the back of a spoon to create a design that resembles swells in the sea. If you'd like, channel your inner Jackson Pollock and splatter with prickly pear syrup, which is made by simmering prickly pear with a little sugar and water until nice and sticky.

In Mexico, the pairing of chocolate and chile goes back hundreds of years. No news there. But the avocado buttercream is a new innovation. The avocado gives the frosting a really interesting vegetal note, and probably some nutritional value, yet it's so rich it's like throwing in an extra stick of butter. Chill the frosted cake before serving to allow the buttercream to set. At Hartwood, we bake the cake in a cast–iron skillet, but this recipe is for cake pans.

This cake is quite spicy—you may want to use less chile powder the first time you make it.   SERVES 8

CHOCOLATE HABANERO CAKE with CHOCOLATE AVOCADO BUTTERCREAM

CAKE

2 cups all-purpose flour

2 cups sugar

¾ cup unsweetened cocoa powder

2 teaspoons baking powder

1½ teaspoons baking soda

1 teaspoon kosher salt

1 tablespoon finely ground coffee

1 tablespoon ground cinnamon

½ teaspoon ground allspice

½ teaspoon ancho chile powder, or to taste

½ teaspoon chipotle chile powder, or to taste

¼ teaspoon habanero powder, or to taste

1¼ cups whole milk

¼ cup vegetable oil

2 large eggs

2 teaspoons vanilla extract

BUTTERCREAM

6 ounces unsweetened chocolate, chopped

½ pound (2 sticks) unsalted butter, cubed, softened

1 ripe Hass avocado, halved, pitted, peeled, and cut into chunks

1 teaspoon vanilla extract

1 cup confectioners' sugar, sifted

Make the cake: Preheat the oven to 350°F. Grease two 9-inch round cake pans. Line the bottoms and sides with parchment paper and grease the parchment. Set aside.

Whisk the flour, sugar, cocoa powder, baking powder, baking soda, salt, coffee, cinnamon, allspice, and chile powders together in a medium bowl.

Whisk together the milk, oil, eggs, and vanilla in a large bowl until thoroughly combined. Fold in the flour mixture, mixing until smooth.

Pour the batter into the cake pans and bake for 45 minutes, or until a toothpick or tester inserted in the center of a layer comes out clean. Set on wire racks to cool for 10 minutes, then turn out of the pans onto racks, remove the parchment paper, and cool completely.

Make the buttercream: Melt the chocolate slowly in the top of a double boiler set over medium-low heat. Set aside to cool to room temperature.

With a handheld electric mixer, beat the butter in a medium bowl until fluffy. Beat in the avocado and vanilla. Slowly add the confectioners' sugar, beating until fully combined. Add the cooled chocolate, mixing until fully incorporated.

Put one cake layer on a serving plate and frost the top. Top with second layer and frost the top and sides of the cake. Refrigerate until ready to serve.

The coconut palms growing on the beach in Tulum are miraculous trees. Even though they're battered by the salty air and exposed to the harsh sun, they still produce fruit filled with a slightly sweet water that's as refreshing as it is healthy and a sweet milky flesh you can eat raw.

At Hartwood, we use fresh coconuts for this cake, but that's a hard recipe to put down on paper. The coconuts here are harvested every day—you're simply not going to find the same quality in a store. So instead we call for cream of coconut, which is a perfectly legitimate substitution. Just be sure to stir the contents of the can before measuring it out.   SERVES 8 TO 10

TOASTED-COCONUT CAKE

CAKE

½ cup coconut oil

3 cups all-purpose flour

1 teaspoon baking soda

¾ teaspoon kosher salt

2 cups sugar

8 tablespoons (1 stick) unsalted butter, softened

3 large eggs

2 large egg yolks

1 cup well-stirred sweetened cream of coconut (such as Coco López)

¾ cup plain whole-milk yogurt

2 teaspoons vanilla extract

FROSTING

Two 8-ounce packages cream cheese, softened

½ cup confectioners' sugar

¼ cup water, or as needed

1 tablespoon dark rum

½ teaspoon fresh lime juice

½ teaspoon vanilla extract

Pinch of salt

1 cup unsweetened coconut flakes, and 1 cup shredded coconut, toasted until golden brown

Preheat the oven to 325°F. Liberally grease two 9-inch springform pans with 2 tablespoons each of the coconut oil; set aside.

Sift the flour, baking soda, and salt into a medium bowl; set aside.

Using a handheld electric mixer, cream the sugar, butter, and the remaining ¼ cup coconut oil in a large bowl until well blended, about 3 minutes (it will look like wet sand). Add the eggs and yolks one at a time, beating well after each addition, then beat for an additional 2 minutes. Beat in the cream of coconut, yogurt, and vanilla. Add the flour mixture, mixing on low just to blend.

Pour the batter into the prepared pans. Gently shake the pans from side to side to smooth the tops. Bake for about 1 hour, or until the top of the cake is golden and a toothpick or tester inserted into the center comes out clean. Remove from the oven and let cool in the pans on a wire rack for 30 minutes.

Run a thin knife around the sides of the pans and remove the pan sides. Let the cake cool completely before frosting.

Make the frosting: Using a handheld electric mixer, beat the cream cheese and confectioners' sugar on medium-low speed until light and creamy, about 3 minutes. Beat in the water, rum, lime juice, vanilla, and salt until blended; add more water, 1 teaspoon at a time, if the frosting is too thick.

Put one cake layer on a serving plate and frost the top. Put the second layer on top and frost the top and sides of the cake. Sprinkle some toasted coconut flakes on top and gently press the rest into the sides.

This cake gets its moistness from coconut oil and yogurt. You want it to be so creamy that when you cut it into slices, it's right on the edge between cake and custard.

One of the keys to the flavor is grilling the pineapple first. If you don't want to start a fire just for dessert, plan ahead: The next time you're grilling for dinner, throw on the pineapple while the flames are still high. Then make the cake in the next few days.   SERVES 8

GRILLED PINEAPPLE UPSIDE-DOWN CAKE

PINEAPPLE

½ ripe pineapple (about 1½ pounds), cut horizontally

1 tablespoon kosher salt

3½ tablespoons sugar

½ cup pineapple juice

CARAMEL

8 tablespoons (1 stick) unsalted butter

4 ounces (½ cone) piloncillo

½ teaspoon kosher salt

CAKE

3 tablespoons coconut oil

1½ cups all-purpose flour

½ teaspoon baking soda

½ teaspoon kosher salt

1 cup sugar

4 tablespoons (½ stick) unsalted butter, softened

2 large eggs

1 large egg yolk

1 cup plain whole-milk yogurt

1 teaspoon vanilla extract

Candied Jamaica Flowers (recipe follows) for garnish

Prepare a grill for high heat.

Peel the pineapple (if you have a pineapple corer, core it now). Cut the pineapple into ⅓-inch-thick slices. Using a small round cutter, cut out the core from each slice. Oil the grill grate. Sprinkle the pineapple slices on both sides with the salt and 2 tablespoons of the sugar and grill until they have good grill marks, about 3 minutes. Turn the slices 45 degrees and grill for 3 more minutes. Flip the slices and repeat. Remove from the heat, transfer to a bowl, and let cool.

Once they are cool, pour the pineapple juice over the grilled pineapple and sprinkle with the remaining 1½ tablespoons sugar.

Make the caramel: Combine the butter, piloncillo, salt, and a splash of the pineapple juice from the bowl with the pineapple in a saucepan and cook over medium heat, stirring occasionally, until the piloncillo is completely melted and a deep amber caramel has formed. (Time will vary according to the piloncillo.)

Meanwhile, arrange the pineapple slices in the bottom of the prepared cake pan. Drink the remaining pineapple juice (it's great in a cocktail).

Make the cake: Preheat the oven to 350°F. Grease a 10-inch springform pan with 1 tablespoon of the coconut oil. Line the sides and bottom with parchment paper and grease the parchment. Set aside.

Sift the flour, baking soda, and salt into a medium bowl; set aside.

Using a handheld electric mixer on medium speed, cream the sugar, butter, and the remaining 2 tablespoons coconut oil in a large bowl until well blended, about 3 minutes (it will look like wet sand). Add the eggs and yolk one at a time, beating well after each addition, then beat for an additional 2 minutes. Beat in the yogurt and vanilla. Beat in the flour mixture on low speed, just to blend.

Pour the caramel evenly over the pineapple slices, then pour the batter evenly over the caramel. Bake for 40 minutes, or until a toothpick or tester inserted into the center of cake (but not into the pineapple) comes out clean. Let the cake cool to room temperature in the pan on a wire rack.

To serve, place a serving plate on top of the pan and, in one quick motion, holding both plate and pan, flip over the cake. Remove the sides of the pan, then remove the pan bottom and peel off the parchment paper. Garnish with candied jamaica flowers.

CANDIED JAMAICA FLOWERS

MAKES 2 CUPS

Candied jamaica flowers, chewy but light and delicious, give a tart taste to a sweet dessert.

2 cups dried jamaica
(hibiscus) flowers

¾ cup sugar

Pinch of kosher salt

Combine the jamaica flowers and water to cover generously in a medium saucepan, bring to a simmer, and cook over low heat for about 30 minutes, until the flowers have softened. Strain the jamaica flowers and spread on paper towels to drain briefly.

Put the flowers in a bowl and toss with the sugar and salt to coat. Heat a large cast-iron skillet over high heat until hot. Add the sugared flowers and stir with a fork until the sugar melts and the flowers are lightly coated with syrup, about 2 minutes. Remove from the heat and transfer the flowers to a sheet of parchment paper to cool. Once they are cool, place the flowers in an airtight container and store in the freezer; they will not freeze hard.

Brûléed grapefruit slices garnish our Grapefruit, Mezcal, and Burnt Honey Cake. Sometimes we cut the burnt parchment paper into squares and use them as serving plates.

This cake is smoky and moist. The grapefruit holds the smokiness of the mezcal so that the flavor permeates the entire cake without overdoing it—you taste a little bit of everything in each bite, all the flavors in balance. SERVES 8 TO 10

GRAPEFRUIT, MEZCAL, and BURNT HONEY CAKE

CAKE

3½ cups all-purpose flour

¼ cup ground cinnamon

1 teaspoon baking soda

½ teaspoon baking powder

Pinch of salt

½ pound (2 sticks) unsalted butter, cubed, softened

1 cup sugar

3 large eggs

1 tablespoon vanilla extract

1½ cups plain whole-milk yogurt

¼ cup sweetened condensed milk

1 cup dark honey

2 grapefruit, suprêmed (see page 45; zest the grapefruit first for the caramel and then squeeze the juice from the membranes as well)

CARAMEL

1 cup water

½ cup sugar

¼ cup grapefruit juice (reserved from the grapefruits you suprêmed)

2 tablespoons mezcal

¼ cup dark honey

1 tablespoon grated grapefruit zest (from the grapefruits you suprêmed)

2 tablespoons unsalted butter

Confectioner's sugar for dusting (optional)

Preheat the oven to 350°F. Butter a 9-inch round cake pan; line with baking parchment and butter the parchment.

Whisk together the flour, cinnamon, baking soda, baking powder, and salt in a medium bowl.

Using a handheld electric mixer, cream the butter and sugar in a large bowl until light and fluffy. Add the eggs one at a time, mixing well after each addition, then add the vanilla and mix to combine. Add the yogurt, sweetened condensed milk, and ¾ cup of the honey and mix to combine. Mix the dry ingredients into the wet ingredients, being careful not to overmix.

Arrange the grapefruit suprêmes in concentric rings in the bottom of the cake pan. Pour the remaining ¼ cup honey over the grapefruit. Pour the batter into the pan. Bake for 45 minutes, or until a cake tester inserted into the center comes out clean. Transfer the pan to a rack and let cool.

Make the caramel: Combine the water and sugar in a medium saucepan, bring to a simmer, and simmer until the sugar melts and the caramel turns a dark amber color. (Be careful at the end—it can burn quickly.) Add the grapefruit juice (the caramel will bubble up) and swirl to incorporate, then add the mezcal and continue swirling until the caramel returns to a dark amber. Add the honey, grapefruit zest, and butter and swirl to incorporate, then take off the heat.

At Hartwood, we brûlée the top of the cake by putting the pan on the grill, grapefruit side down, for 3 to 4 minutes, so that the grapefruit and honey turn golden brown and crisp up. You probably won't do that, but if you want the same effect, invert the cake onto a rack, peel off the parchment, and brown the top with a blowtorch. Or set it under a preheated broiler for 1 to 2 minutes, until bubbly and browned.

If you have not already done so, invert the cake onto a cooling rack and remove the paper. Transfer the cake to a serving plate and pour over the warm caramel. Sprinkle with confectioners' sugar, if desired.

Our take on banana pudding. This is made with overripe plátanos machos—large, sweet bananas left to mature until the skin is almost entirely black and the flesh tastes a little fermented. (If you can't find plátanos machos at a Mexican market or other specialty store, you can substitute super-ripe bananas.) The pudding has a pronounced flavor of vanilla, which is intentional—vanilla originated in Mexico, where it was cultivated on the west coast, then taken to other regions by the Aztecs. The vanilla pod is the fruit of an orchid that grows on a vine and that flowers for just one day. The green pods are dried in the sun until dark and sweet. Something to think about the next time you use the word "vanilla" to describe something flat and flavorless. SERVES 8

YUCATÁN PLÁTANO PUDDING

3 large very ripe bananas (not peeled)

5 large eggs

½ cup sugar

¼ cup cornstarch (if you can get arrowroot powder, even better)

¼ teaspoon salt

4 cups whole milk

2 large vanilla beans

2 tablespoons unsalted butter

½ cup sour cream

3 tablespoons dark honey, plus extra for drizzling

Preheat the oven to 400°F. Line a rimmed baking sheet with foil.

Put the bananas on the baking sheet and roast for 40 to 45 minutes, until blackened and beginning to caramelize at the ends (they will also start to caramelize on the inside). Remove from the oven and let cool, then peel.

Whisk the eggs, sugar, cornstarch, and salt together in a medium bowl.

Pour the milk into a medium saucepan set over medium-low heat. Split the vanilla beans in half and scrape the seeds into the milk, then add the pods. Bring to a gentle simmer, being careful not to scorch the milk. Remove from the heat and remove the vanilla pods, scraping out any remaining seeds before discarding them.

Gradually whisk about one-quarter of the warm milk mixture into the eggs, then whisk in the rest of the milk.

Quickly clean the saucepan and return the egg mixture to it. Set a large bowl in an ice bath.

Set the saucepan over medium heat and whisk constantly until the pudding is thickened, about 4 minutes. Whisk in the butter and then one of the bananas in large chunks, until smooth (the pudding will be slightly chunky because of the banana—this is okay). Transfer to the bowl set in the ice bath and stir gently until cool, then place plastic wrap directly on the surface so a skin does not form, place in the refrigerator, and chill completely, about 2 hours.

Coarsely chop the remaining 2 roasted bananas, saving some pieces. Gently whisk the pudding to loosen it slightly, then fold in the sour cream, honey, and bananas.

Spoon the pudding into bowls and drizzle with honey, and garnish with the reserved pieces of roasted bananas.

When life gives you limes—crates and crates of limes—you find new ways to use them in dessert, like this beachfront interpretation of the French lemon tart. This is a classic recipe, with all the butter and eggs you'd find in its Parisian counterpart. We roast lime wedges while the tart bakes, for a caramelized sweet-tart garnish. SERVES 8

LIME TART with LIME CARAMEL

CRUST

12 tablespoons (1½ sticks) unsalted butter, softened

¼ cup sugar

2 cups all-purpose flour

¼ teaspoon salt

1 teaspoon dried chamomile or organic chamomile tea

LIME CURD

3 large eggs

4 large egg yolks

1 cup sugar

1 tablespoon grated lime zest (from about 3 limes)

¾ cup fresh lime juice (from 8 to 9 large limes)

¼ teaspoon salt

8 tablespoons (1 stick) unsalted butter, cut into chunks, softened

LIME CARAMEL

1 cone piloncillo (about 8 ounces), chopped

¼ cup fresh lime juice (from 2 to 3 limes)

1 teaspoon kosher salt

4 tablespoons unsalted butter, softened

1 lime, halved, sliced into thin wedges, and roasted until slightly charred (optional)

Dried chamomile or organic chamomile tea for garnish

Zest of 1 lime for garnish

Make the crust: Using a handheld electric mixer, cream the butter and sugar together in a medium bowl until light and fluffy. Add the flour, salt, and chamomile and mix until a dough forms. Shape into a flat disk and wrap in plastic wrap. Chill for 30 minutes, or until firm.

Preheat the oven to 400°F.

Press the dough evenly into the bottom and up the sides of a 9-inch tart pan. Use a fork to poke holes all over it so that the crust doesn't bubble while baking. Bake until lightly golden brown, about 15 minutes. Transfer to a wire rack to cool completely. Reduce the oven temperature to 350°F.

Make the curd: Fill a saucepan about halfway with water and heat it over medium-low heat until simmering. Meanwhile, in a heatproof bowl that you can set over the saucepan, whisk together the eggs, yolks, and sugar. Set the bowl over the saucepan and continue whisking until the sugar is dissolved, about 1 minute. Add the lime zest, juice, and salt and cook, stirring constantly, until the mixture is thick enough to coat the back of the spoon, about 4 minutes. Make sure to scrape down the sides frequently so that the curd does not overcook. Whisk in the butter piece by piece.

Pour the curd into the crust. Bake for 15 to 20 minutes, or until the filling is set. Let cool completely, then refrigerate until cold and set, at least 3 hours. (The tart can be refrigerated for up to 3 days.)

Make the caramel: Melt the piloncillo with the lime juice and salt in a saucepan over medium heat until completely fluid, stirring to break up any stubborn pieces. Stir in the butter and remove from the heat. Let cool.

To serve, remove the sides of the pan, cut the tart into wedges, and arrange on serving plates. (We bake ours in trays and then slice them into squares.) Top each serving with a drizzle of caramel, a few roasted lime wedges, if using, a sprinkle of chamomile, and a pinch of lime zest.

If Mexico had an official national dessert, it would be flan, that creamy custard served in a shallow pool of a thin caramel sauce. It's almost always good, or at least satisfying, but it's hardly ever great. The challenge was to create a version of a familiar dish that tastes new while remaining true to tradition. We don't do much to the flan, but we infuse the caramel with chamomile to give it a faintly herbaceous flavor, then garnish it with candied peanuts (which you see in all the markets here), because it's nice to have a little crunch in every bite.

SERVES 6

CHAMOMILE FLAN with CANDIED PEANUTS

FLAN

1 cup whole milk

1 cup heavy cream

5 large eggs

¼ teaspoon kosher salt

1 tablespoon honey

½ cup sugar

2 tablespoons water

1½ teaspoons dried chamomile or organic chamomile tea

CANDIED PEANUTS

1 cup raw peanuts

¾ cup sugar

2 tablespoons water

½ teaspoon kosher salt

Organic chamomile flowers for garnish (optional)

Make the flan: Preheat the oven to 300°F. Set out six 6- to 8-ounce ramekins.

Whisk the milk, cream, eggs, salt, and honey in a bowl; set aside.

Combine the sugar and water in a small heavy saucepan and bring to a simmer over medium heat, stirring until the sugar dissolves. Stop stirring and simmer, swirling the pan occasionally, until the mixture is a dark golden brown caramel, make sure it doesn't burn. Remove from the heat, stir in the chamomile, and immediately pour a tablespoon or so of caramel into each ramekin. Add the custard mixture.

Place the ramekins in a baking dish. Fill the dish with water to come about halfway up the sides of the ramekins. Cover the dish with aluminum foil, place in the oven, and cook for about 50 minutes. Check the flan—it should barely wiggle. If not set, bake for another 10 to 15 minutes. Remove from the water bath and let cool slightly.

Meanwhile, make the candied peanuts: Combine the peanuts, sugar, and water in a medium saucepan and bring to a boil over medium-high heat. Lower the heat to medium and cook, stirring every minute or so, until the sugar becomes powdery. Add the salt and continue to cook, stirring every couple of minutes, until the mixture remelts. (Patience! It can take up to 15 minutes.) Once all the sugar has dissolved and evenly coats the now-roasted peanuts, remove from the heat and spread out on a sheet of parchment to cool.

Break the candied peanuts apart with your hands.

To serve, run an offset spatula or table knife around the edge of each flan to loosen it, place a small plate on top of the ramekin, and quickly invert to unmold the flan; the caramel will spill out. Garnish with the candied peanuts and chamomile flowers, if using.

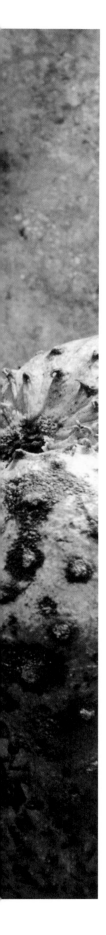

Guanabana fruit (soursop) has a natural creaminess that makes this recipe seem like a cheat: simply mash the flesh, freeze it, and scoop it into bowls, and it will seem as if you made a perfectly tempered custard. In fact, this dish was discovered by accident: somebody left a guanabana in the freezer, and somebody else decided to eat it. It's important to use a very ripe guanabana, which you touch up with just a little bit of honey (for sweetness) and season with a pinch of salt (to bring the flavors into focus). The fruit has large, shiny black seeds that you don't need to remove—they're easy to eat around, and they give the dessert a rustic feel.   SERVES 4

ICY
GUANABANA

1 ripe guanabana (about the size of
    a cantaloupe)
2 tablespoons light honey
Pinch of kosher salt

Halve the guanabana and scoop out the flesh, leaving the seeds intact. Mash in a bowl with a spoon. Mix in the honey and salt. Transfer to a baking pan or dish and freeze overnight.

To serve, use an ice cream scoop to scrape up the frozen fruit and place in serving bowls.

Every so often, Viviana Lopez Mendez, the head of prep, will bring in a batch of sweet tamales that she has made at home. They don't go on the menu—they're for the staff, who devour them the moment they come out of the steamer. These are straight-up sweet, although this recipe reduces the amount of sugar Vivi uses to account for the sweeter corn you get in the United States. The basics are simple, but you might need some practice folding the corn husks.

MAKES ABOUT 12 TAMALES

SWEET FRESH-CORN TAMALES

10 to 12 ears corn, husked and cleaned of silk, reserving about 30 tender light green leaves for wrapping the tamales

One 14-ounce can sweetened condensed milk

1 cup sugar

¼ cup ground cinnamon

Use a chef's knife to cut the kernels off the corn cobs. Run the kernels through a food mill fitted with a fine plate. Put the corn puree in a fine-mesh strainer set over a bowl and let the excess liquid drain, about 5 minutes.

Transfer the corn to another bowl and mix in the sweetened condensed milk, sugar, and cinnamon.

Place a corn husk on the counter with the pointed end away from you. Spoon ¾ cup of the corn mixture into the middle, just slightly off center toward the flat side. Snugly fold over the two long flaps, almost like you're folding a business letter, then fold over 3 to 4 inches of the pointed end of the husk. (You want to make sure that there's some tension, or it will be too flat.) Pick up the package and hold it like a cup, with the folded side toward you, being careful that none of the corn mixture spills out, then take a second leaf, and, with the wide end on top, and repeat the process: snugly fold over the two long flaps, then fold over the flat end. Finally, tuck the flap under like a pocket. If necessary, cut a long thin strip from a corn husk and use it to tie the tamale closed. Repeat with the remaining filling and husks.

Place a bamboo steamer basket on top of a large pot of boiling water. Carefully lay the tamales in the steamer in a single layer (you will probably need to do this in batches). Cover the steamer basket and cook the tamales for 20 minutes, until slightly firm. Serve warm.

Adelsy and Viviana
discuss how many
tamales to make (and
how many will get eaten
while they make them).

EL CON PANAL

IEL CON POLEN

IEL CON PROPO

LEA REAL

OLEN. CREMA DI

ARAMELO DE I

RON DE MIEI

Las Bebidas

DRINKS

Fresh, flavorful, and not too sweet—
that's the polestar that guides the drinks
at Hartwood. Every cocktail should be
seductive and tasty, but it should also
be refreshing and prepare you for what
you're about to eat—or for another
drink—rather than fill you up or shut
down your palate for the night.

Almost all of our drinks are built on
the fresh fruit juices we prepare every
day in the prep kitchen: nothing is ever
poured out of a box, or bought from one
of the juice stands in town, or saved
from the night before. No way. The fruit
we juice depends on the fruit in the
market, so the drinks change with the
seasons. Every day, we sort through the
fruit to pick out what is at peak ripeness,
and every afternoon we clamp the juicer
to the side of the prep table and plug the

blender into the socket (and hope it's working). Then we start juicing.

The spirit of choice is mezcal, which is made by fermenting the hearts of smoked agave plants. The best-known kind of mezcal is tequila. (Mezcal is a category of spirits, like whiskey, while tequila is a subcategory, like bourbon.) The mention of the word scares off some, which is too bad—a good mezcal is as delicious as a fine Cognac. We stock different kinds at the bar, including one beautiful mezcal that is delivered in plastic jerry cans that were carried down a mountain by pack mules. But you can put most mezcals in one of two categories: intensely smoky ones that stand up to strong flavors, and subtler ones that are best in more delicate cocktails. We specify which kind is best for each drink in these recipes.

The night sky in Tulum is filled with stars, and when you look up, you can see the constellations, maybe a meteor shower. You're always aware of the cosmos—even the streets in town have astral names: Centauro, Andromeda, Polar Ponte—so when we first made this drink and watched the deep purple of the hibiscus infusion gently float through the mezcal and mandarin orange juice, we thought it looked like a supernova in a glass. It makes a stunning first impression when you set it down. The choice of mezcal is important: you want it strong and smoky so the flavor comes through the sweetness of the mandarin juice. A mild mezcal will disappear.

MAKES 1 DRINK

SUPERNOVA

1 cup fresh mandarin orange juice (or regular orange juice)

1 shot smoky mezcal

1 tablespoon brewed jamaica (hibiscus) tea (brewed from 1 teabag or loose dried hibiscus flowers), chilled

2 slices lime, for garnish

Fill a glass with ice. Pour in the orange juice and mezcal and stir to combine. Gently pour in the hibiscus tea so that it stains the top of the drink and slowly filters through the orange juice. Garnish with the lime slices.

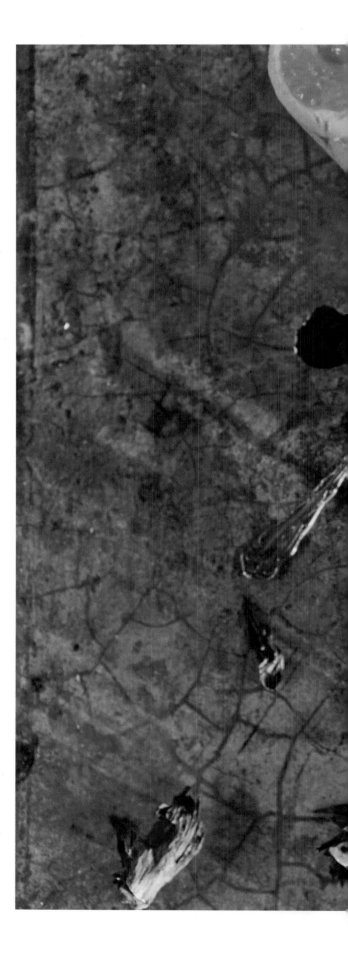

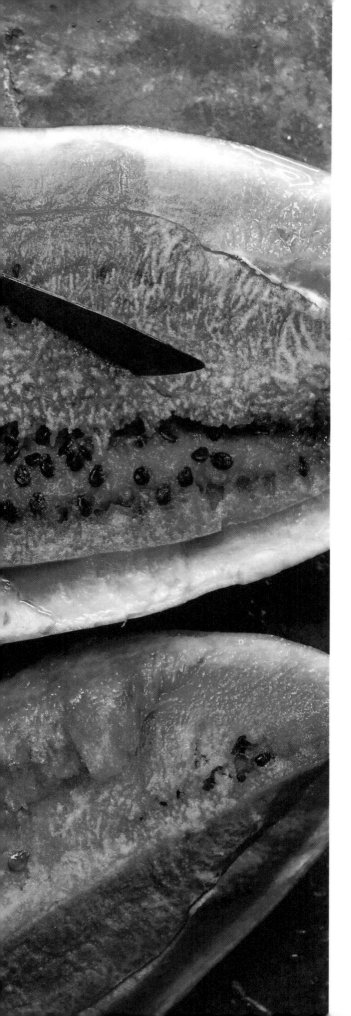

We see so many couples here who are obviously really into each other. It's funny that a drink name can have an effect on their night, but it seems to do just that—couples love to order this drink. The name is a more decorous play on Sex on the Beach. If you can make fresh passion fruit juice, do it, because the sweet-tart flavor of the fruit is so distinctive. (Puree the pulp in a blender, then strain; 1 cup pulp will yield ½ cup juice.) You can tell if somebody has made it fresh, because the juice will be flecked with tiny fragments of seeds; the boxed stuff is pure orange. Now you know.   MAKES 1 DRINK

PASSION IN THE JUNGLE

¼ cup mint leaves, roughly torn

1 teaspoon sugar

¼ cup passion fruit juice,
    preferably fresh

2 tablespoons fresh orange juice

1 shot white rum

1 tablespoon fresh watermelon juice
    (puree chunks of watermelon in a blender, then strain)

An 8-inch strip of sugarcane for garnish (optional)

Combine the mint and sugar in a glass and muddle with a bar spoon. Add the passion fruit juice, and orange juice, and stir. Fill the glass with ice and pour in the rum and then the watermelon juice, so that it floats on the top of the drink. Garnish with the sugarcane, if desired.

Our signature drink: it's refreshing and, because it's not too sweet, you can easily drink more than one. The secret is the aromatic, spicy ginger juice. (If you don't have a juicer, blend fresh ginger with a little water and strain the liquid through a fine sieve.) The sharp bite balances the other flavors.

MAKES 1 DRINK

THE
HARTWOOD

1 tablespoon fresh lime juice

3 slices (about ¼ inch thick) ginger

1 teaspoon Ginger Simple Syrup (recipe follows)

½ teaspoon ginger juice (see headnote)

1 shot whiskey, preferably Jameson

Club soda to top

A thin lime slice for garnish

Fill a glass with ice. Add the lime juice, ginger, simple syrup, ginger juice, and whis-key and stir to combine. Top off with club soda and garnish with the lime slice.

GINGER SIMPLE SYRUP

MAKES ¼ CUP

Leftover ginger syrup is delicious mixed with soda water, or stir it into iced tea or lemonade.

¼ cup sugar

¼ cup water

1 ounce ginger, thinly sliced

Combine the sugar, water, and ginger in a small saucepan and bring to a boil over medium-high heat. Lower the temperature and simmer for 5 minutes. Remove from the heat and let cool to room temperature, then strain.

Thick, fruity, spicy: this is a margarita with a lot of personality. It's also a drink best made in batches. If you do your prep ahead of time (infuse the tequila with the habanero 36 hours before; puree fresh pineapple in a blender earlier in the day), you can mix together one round after another after your guests arrive. A trick from behind the bar: Shake the drink and pour two-thirds of it into the glass, then shake the rest of the drink again before topping it off, so that the margarita has a slightly frothy head.   MAKES 1 DRINK

PIÑA-HABANERO MARGARITA

Table salt

Chile Lime Salt (page 100)

1 scant shot tequila reposado

½ shot Habanero Tequila

½ shot Cointreau

½ cup pineapple puree (or substitute fresh pineapple juice)

Pour some table salt onto a small plate and the chile lime salt onto another one. Moisten the rim of a glass and roll it in the table salt, then in the chile salt.

Combine all the liquor and the pineapple puree in a cocktail shaker filled with ice and shake vigorously. Pour into the glass (see headnote) and serve.

HABANERO TEQUILA

4 ounces tequila reposada, 100% agave   1 habanero, halved

Combine the tequila and habanero in a jar, seal tightly, and let infuse for 36 hours. (You can go as little as 24 hours, or as long as 48 hours, depending on how much heat you want.)

Remove the habanero and reseal the jar.

BEHIND THE BAR
Number of different juices
made for the bar by hand
each day: 12
Number of people
required to make them: 4
Number of blenders
available: 1
Number of blenders
that have broken, been
dropped, or rusted in the
salt air: at least 30

You shed your clothes when you're in Tulum. In part it's because of the beach and the heat, but it's also the spirit of the place. When you're here, you want to wear as little as possible, or nothing at all: you want to be *desnudo*. The fresh fruit purees in this drink taste like vacation—you barely notice the rum, which is exactly the idea. MAKES 1 DRINK

DESNUDO

8 mint leaves, roughly torn

1 teaspoon honey

Dash of fresh lime juice

½ shot guanabana puree (passion fruit puree can be substituted)

1 teaspoon coconut water

1 shot white rum

1 shot prickly pear puree

An 8-inch strip of sugarcane for garnish (optional)

Combine the mint, honey, lime juice, guanabana puree, and coconut water in a glass, then fill the glass with ice. Add the rum and top off with the prickly pear puree. Garnish with the sugarcane stalk, if desired.

Our homage to the vodka watermelon, that underage trick of pouring a bottle of vodka into a watermelon and then eating it at a barbecue as if it were an innocent piece of fruit. The flavors here are pure and clean: watermelon, mint, a slice of cucumber to munch on as you drink. When produce is good, you truly don't need to do too much to it.   MAKES 1 DRINK

SANDIA
LOCA

8 mint leaves, roughly torn

1 shot vodka

½ cup fresh watermelon juice (puree chunks of watermelon in a blender, then strain)

A sprig of mint for garnish

Put the mint leaves in a glass and muddle them with a bar spoon, then fill the glass with ice. Add the vodka and watermelon juice. Garnish with the sprig of mint.

A fresh, summery drink that's a play on the classic Gin–Gin Mule. There's just a hint of sweetness, which is exactly the idea. The flavors here are strong, but they keep each other in balance—go too far with the ginger, or the honey, or the lime, though, and the flavor will tilt too far to one side. You can easily make this by the pitcher.   MAKES 1 DRINK

GIN-GIN
QUEEN

3 slices ginger

10 mint leaves, roughly torn

1 tablespoon fresh lime juice

1 teaspoon honey

1 shot gin

Club soda to top

Pomegranate seeds for garnish

Combine the ginger, mint, lime juice, and honey in a glass and muddle with a bar spoon—you want to stir with enthusiasm, even a little aggression, but you're not out to hurt anybody. Fill the glass with ice. Add the gin, then fill to the top with club soda. Garnish with pomegranate seeds.

You can ask for chaya to be thrown into any of the drinks you get at the juice bars in town, which isn't as hippieish as it might seem. You drink juice here the way you sip wine in Paris. Chaya's mild, spinach-like green leaves are rich in antioxidants, so it's like the proverbial apple a day—you eat it because you know it does your body good. The vodka hides in this drink, so it tastes more like something you might order after a swim than a cocktail.

To make lemongrass tea, boil 4 to 6 roughly chopped lemongrass stalks in 1 cup water for 1 minute. Let stand for 5 minutes, then strain. Stir in 1 tablespoon honey until dissolved. **MAKES 1 DRINK**

MANTIS

½ cup chaya juice (puree 1 cup
    chaya leaves in a blender with water,
    then strain through a fine-mesh
    sieve; spinach can be substituted)

1 shot lemongrass tea (see headnote)

1 shot vodka

1 shot fresh pineapple puree
    (or pineapple juice)

A pineapple wedge for garnish

Combine the chaya juice, tea, vodka, and pineapple puree in a cocktail shaker and fill with ice. Shake vigorously and pour into a glass. Garnish with the pineapple wedge.

A *marocha* is a woman with dark hair and smoky coloring; it's also slang for a party girl, the one who's always going out and hitting the dance floor. This drink tastes how a marocha looks: earthy papaya (which becomes buttery when pureed) paired with smoky mezcal and brightened with orange juice. It's also what a marocha might drink to get the night going.

MAKES 1 DRINK

MAROCHA

2 shots papaya puree

1 shot smoky mezcal

¼ cup fresh orange juice

Pour the papaya puree into a glass, then fill the glass with ice. Add the mezcal and orange juice and stir well.

MARINE-GRADE VARNISH

Hartwood might nominally be a building, but we maintain it as if it were a ship. Every day, we go around with a bucket of marine-grade varnish (to touch up the tables, chairs, and wood beams), black metal paint (for the iron footrests at the bar, the lanterns, and any other exposed metal fixtures), and a bucket of white paint (to cover the marks on the walls, the trash bins, and the produce crates we use in the kitchen). Several times a day, we sweep the leaves from the overhangs and from the crushed white rocks that make up the floor—which we refresh every few weeks with more rocks. If it rains in the middle of the day, we wipe down all the tables and chairs. If it rains again, we do it again.

Part of this routine is to appease our obsessive natures: we like working in an orderly place. And some of it is because we want the restaurant to look nice. If you're here on vacation and this is your big night out, we want the restaurant to be up to that sense of occasion. But mostly, it's an extreme form of prevention. If we didn't treat the wood and the metal, if we didn't constantly repaint the walls, if we didn't sweep up the leaves, if we let it go for just a little bit, then the jungle would take back the land that is rightfully hers. Within a few days, fungus would start sprouting from the walls and posts; within a week, there would be a layer of soil-like mulch on the ground. Within two weeks, plants would be growing wild; within a month, you wouldn't recognize it.

Not long ago, Tulum was lashed by so many rainstorms that the cenotes started running over—the jungle simply couldn't absorb the water. For a week, the restaurant was filled with standing water that came up above our knees. When it finally drained, the place looked like a car dragged up from the bottom of a lake. We waited until the rains stopped and the water receded, then we set to work. We called in the staff, broke out the brushes and brooms, and bought another case of marine-grade varnish.

A Michelada is one of those classic drinks with a thousand variations, every one of them definitive: the version you make is the right one, and all the others get it wrong. Basically, make a spicy, richly flavored base that tastes like bouillon spiked with Tabasco and lime, pour it into a glass filled with ice, and top off with a dark beer that has just enough backbone to stand up to it. The drink changes minute by minute: you take a sip, the ice melts, you top up the glass with more beer, the Maggi seasoning and Worcestershire sauce become more pronounced. If you use a straw, the drink starts intense and mellows out; if you just drink from the glass, it starts clean and grows more potent. A Michelada is like a frosty, spicy beer soup, which might sound weird, but it's one of the great cocktails of all time. It's best in a glass that has been chilled in the freezer. Brand names matter. You must use Lea & Perrins Worcestershire sauce, Maggi seasoning, and Tabasco.   MAKES 1 DRINK

MICHELADA

Kosher salt

1 teaspoon Worcestershire sauce

½ teaspoon Maggi seasoning

½ teaspoon Tabasco sauce

1 tablespoon fresh lime juice

2 cups crushed ice

One 12–ounce bottle Negra Modelo

A straw for serving

Moisten the rim of a glass and rim with salt. Add the Worcestershire sauce, Maggi seasoning, Tabasco, and lime juice and stir. Add the crushed ice, top off with beer, and insert the straw. Serve with the rest of the bottle of beer on the side.

A Chelada is a streamlined Michelada: lime juice and beer on ice in a glass with a salted rim. A Michelada is a lot of drink, so you might move from a Chelada to a Michelada (or the other way around). Or you might stick with the Chelada. If anybody gives you grief about drinking beer with ice, tell him to relax, go to the beach, and order a Michelada or Chelada, then get back to you.   MAKES 1 DRINK

CHELADA

Kosher salt

1 tablespoon fresh lime juice

2 cups crushed ice

One 12-ounce bottle Negra Modelo

A straw for serving

Moisten the rim of a glass and rim with salt. Add the lime juice and crushed ice, top off with beer, and insert the straw. Serve with the rest of the bottle of beer on the side.

Left: The Chelada
Right: The Michelada

Less cloying than traditional sangria but more flavorful than a *tinto de verano*, that wine-and-soft-drink mix you find in the south of Spain, this is what you want after the beach. It's light, brisk, clean. This recipe is for one drink, but you can certainly make it by the pitcher. We use a dry Chardonnay from Monterey, which produces some excellent wines. You want a crisp Chardonnay with no oaky flavors.

MAKES 1 DRINK

WINE COOLER

20 mint leaves

4 thin slices ginger

1 teaspoon honey

4 mandarin orange or clementine segments

6 to 8 slices peeled cucumber

1 cup Chardonnay

¼ cup soda water

Combine the mint, ginger, and honey in a glass and muddle with a bar spoon. Add ice cubes, the orange segments, cucumber slices, and wine. Top off with the soda water and mix gently with the spoon.

This rice milk is a Mexican standard—it's street food, but you can order it in nice restaurants, or make it at home for special occasions. Usually it's too sweet, though, so we tone down the sugar. We toast the rice in a cast-iron skillet to give it a nutty flavor, and we add a little *pimiento de Tabasco*, which is the market name for *pimiento de Jamaica*—known in the United States as allspice. The zapote seed infuses the drink with an almond flavor; you can substitute whole almonds.

MAKES ABOUT 6 CUPS

HORCHATA

5 cups water

2 cups long-grain white rice

2 cinnamon sticks

1 tablespoon allspice berries

1 zapote negro seed (or substitute
    10 whole almonds)

½ cup sugar, or to taste

Heat the water in a saucepan over low heat just until it is hot.

Meanwhile, put the rice, cinnamon sticks, and allspice berries in a large cast-iron skillet and toast, stirring occasionally, over medium-low heat until the rice is golden and the mixture smells nutty. Remove from the heat and pulverize in a blender until you have a very fine powder. Transfer to a medium bowl.

Pour the warm water over the rice powder. Add the zapote negro seed (or almonds) and sugar. Stir, cover, and refrigerate overnight, or for at least 10 hours.

Remove the zapote negro seed (leave the almonds, if using), transfer the mixture to a blender, and puree until very smooth. Pass through a fine-mesh sieve or a colander lined with cheesecloth into a bowl or other container. Add more cold water if you'd like to make the horchata thinner and more sugar to taste if desired. Cover and refrigerate until ready to serve, or for up to 2 days.

Serve cold over ice.

The breakfast of champions, this is antioxidant–rich and settles your stomach. Don't be intimidated by the aloe verde: it's simple to make a puree out of the paddle of the plant and it's easy to find (most health food stores carry them, as do many specialty shops) and easy to handle (use a vegetable peeler to take off the skin). MAKES 1 DRINK

CHAYA JUICE with ALOE VERDE

1 cup packed chaya leaves (or substitute spinach)

1 cup water

⅓ cup aloe puree (see Note)

1 tablespoon honey

Put the chaya in a blender, add the water, and blend on high speed for 60 seconds. Strain.

Fill a cocktail shaker with the chaya juice, aloe puree, and honey and stir to blend. Add about 1 cup ice cubes, shake well, and strain into an ice–filled glass.

Note: To make aloe puree, take 1 aloe paddle, remove the thorns and skin, and liquefy in a blender.

This drink is named for the state of Campeche to the northwest of Tulum, where pomegranate trees grow wild. While there isn't much to it—fresh pomegranate, honey, water—the drink is delicious, and more elegant and delicate than you might expect. It could also be a base for a cocktail: add a shot of mezcal, and you have a nice drink. You need to make the infusion a day in advance.　MAKES 1 DRINK

CAMPECHE

Seeds from 1 pomegranate (see Note)

½ cup water

2 tablespoons honey

Combine all the ingredients in a jar and refrigerate for 24 hours.

Strain the drink into an ice–filled glass and garnish with a few pomegranate seeds.

Note: Here's an easy way to seed a pomegranate: Cut it in half and score an X into the skin of each half with a chef's knife. Then, working over a bowl, hold one half seed side down in your palm, and use a wooden spoon to smack the scored skin until the seeds shake loose. Pick out any remaining seeds, and repeat with the second half.

LAGOON WORLD

Most visitors don't see the vast flora-and-fauna-filled system of lagoons that stretches many miles inland from the Caribbean, because they're here for the beach. Which is fine, but you're only looking at one thing, and in one direction. Turn around, and you'll see so much more. Sometimes in the afternoon, if we're caught up on prepping for service, or on a Monday, when we're closed but working to catch up for the week, we'll jump in a truck and drive about thirty minutes into the Biosphere, a sprawling protected preserve rich in wildlife.

There's a dock on the lagoon side of the road. From the dock, a boat takes you through the mangroves into a second lagoon, which was part of the ancient Maya trade route. Old stone ruins still mark the way. Then you hop out and float in what's called *agua dulce*, a mixture of saltwater and freshwater. The current takes you through little canals into lagoons that are so mineral-rich that it feels like getting a massage. Is it any wonder we'd rather go here on break than stand in the one spot in front of the restaurant where we can get a bar of cellphone service (if we're lucky) and catch up on e-mail? That can wait until we get home after midnight.

It feels as though a spirit touches you when you stand on the shore of an island in a lagoon. You are reminded that this world has many secrets. Half-fed by cenotes and half-fed by the sea, the lagoons served as trade routes for the Maya thousands of years ago. Just being there is a sacred experience.

The dragon fruit is called *pitaya* around here, and it's a freaky-looking object: the fuchsia skin and rubbery green flaps conceal white flesh that's flecked with tiny black seeds. It tastes like the tropics, bright and fruity and floral, but once you trim away the pink and green, it looks like the sesame seed ice cream you get in Japanese restaurants.

To make this drink, you puree the fruit in a blender—the high water content makes it easy as long as the cubes of fruit are small enough to fall into the whirring blades. In the end, it looks like you have a cup of cake batter. We add a touch of lime juice and honey to wake up the flavors, and the contrast between how it looks and how it tastes is what makes this so much fun to serve.   MAKES 1 DRINK

SWEET LIME DRAGON FRUIT DRINK

½ dragon fruit, peeled and cut into small cubes
2 tablespoons fresh lime juice
2 tablespoons honey
A slice of dragon fruit for garnish
A slice of lime for garnish

Puree the dragon fruit in a blender until loose and liquid. Add the lime juice and honey and pulse to mix. Pour into an ice-filled glass. This actually tastes best after the ice has started to melt.

Garnish with the slices of dragonfruit and lime.

Guanabana has a naturally creamy texture and a slightly citric bite. When you puree the fruit, it's almost as if you have made some complicated smoothie with a half-dozen ingredients—it tastes like a composition. That's why you don't need to do too much to it. A little honey, a little ground allspice to give it depth, and you have a refreshing, satisfying juice that won't fill you up.   MAKES 1 DRINK

GUANABANA HONEY WATER

½ cup guanabana pulp

1 tablespoon honey

½ cup water

¼ teaspoon ground allspice

½ cup ice cubes

Annona leaf for garnish

Pulse the guanabana, honey, water, and allspice in blender, adding the ice one cube at a time to chill. Pour into a glass and garnish with the annona leaf.

Think of this as an energy drink that happens to taste really good. If you have a few too many cocktails or beers one night, try this the next day.

This is a messy drink. The chile flakes on the rim that are supposed to fall into the glass end up on your fingers. It's more fun that way.
MAKES 1 DRINK

AGUA de COCO y CHILE

1 coconut

2 tablespoons honey

2 dried árbol chiles, toasted in a dry skillet until fragrant and ground (reserve ¼ teaspoon for rimming the glass)

1 árbol chile for garnish

Crack the top of the coconut with a machete to create an opening. Add honey and dried chiles and shake vigorously. Pour over ice into a glass rimmed with the reserved ground chile and garnish with the whole chile.

Tepache is a fermented drink you make by soaking the rind of a pineapple for a week. It's best consumed ice–cold on a hot day. MAKES 3 QUARTS

TEPACHE

Rind of 1 large pineapple, cut into 3 to 4 pieces
1½ tablespoons crumbled or crushed piloncillo
3 quarts water
4 cloves

Place the pineapple rind in a resealable 4–quart plastic container, sprinkle with the piloncillo, and toss to coat. Place in direct sunshine for 7 hours. Add the water and cloves, cover, and shake vigorously. Poke 8 pin–size holes in the top of the container to allow air to escape as the drink ferments. Leave in the shade for 1 week (you can put it on the floor of a cool closet) and shake at least once a day.

Strain the tepache and chill in the refrigerator. Serve over ice.

Lemonade is a barbecue standby, but we don't have lemons in the Yucatán, we have limes. This is the tropical version of that tall glass of lemonade you want while working the grill. We use honey because it has a rounder flavor than sugar. Sometimes you need a lot of sweetener to balance the acidic bite of the limes, but when you use granulated sugar, it can become too much. We salt the rims of the glasses not only to honor the salt-and-lime flavorings added to Mexican drinks, but also to play up the sweetness. The pureed mango will soften it even more and allows you to use less honey.

MAKES FOUR 8-OUNCE GLASSES

LIMEADE

6 tablespoons honey

3⅓ cups water

⅔ cup fresh lime juice (from 6 to 7 limes)

1½ teaspoons grated lime zest

Table salt

4 lime slices for garnish

Combine the honey, water, and lime juice and zest in a small pitcher and stir until the honey is dissolved.

Pour some salt onto a saucer, moisten the rim of each glass, and dip into the salt. Put ¼ cup of ice cubes into each glass, fill with limeade, and garnish with a slice of lime.

MANGO LIMEADE

2 ripe mangoes, peeled and pitted

2 cups water

3 tablespoons honey

Grated zest of 1 lime

½ cup fresh lime juice

4 lime slices for garnish

Puree the mangoes in a blender. (You might need to add 1 cup of the water at this point, depending on the ripeness of the fruit.) Pour the puree into a pitcher and add the honey, lime zest and juice, and the (remaining) water. Stir until the honey is dissolved. Pour into ice-filled glasses and garnish with the lime slices.

EPILOGUE

When we opened in 2010, we risked everything in order to have a slower, simpler, more meaningful life and do exactly what we love. Little did we know that in our attempt to take control of our days (and our food), we signed ourselves up to lose control—powerless to the climate, to the needs of the restaurant, and to the complexities of running a business in a foreign country.

We were surrounded on three sides by a sprawling jungle that made us feel ant-sized, and that faced the vastness of the ocean. We were newcomers in a five-thousand-year-old civilization. If we ever thought that we could teach people some New York City tricks, well, we're the ones who are still being educated every day.

When visitors tell us that it must be incredible to live in paradise, we occasionally have to tell them that on some days we refer to our life here as "paradise black hole." There have been tough but important lessons. We've learned never to assume—that the shrimp delivery will come a few hours before service, or that the blender will work, or that it won't pour in the middle of service on New Year's Eve. We've been taught to slow down and look and listen and try to just be, because, as hokey as it sounds, once you realize you're powerless, you're on the road to freedom (even if that road has a police checkpoint). Just as at the markets, where everyone's prices are the same, we've learned to value all things equally and fairly. And we've learned a lot about the fierce physical labor required to prevent our perfectly whitewashed open-air restaurant from being overrun by nature. After a couple of years, your body learns to get used to standing in front of an 800-degree oven and a waist-height grill. You stop burning your forearms and singeing your beard—though in summer, you still have to walk around with a bag of ice on your back for a few minutes every hour to cool down.

Years later, we have a restaurant that supports over twenty employees and countless farmers and fishermen. But we still haven't had time to get business cards printed. (Did we mention that Mya got pregnant right after we opened?) We're not even sure how we found time to write down the recipes for this book. But we're honored to be able to share our food and our story. We hope that you too have found inspiration between the land and the sea.

TRUE COMMUNITY

To us, this means a group of people with something in common. It can be the area where they live, or the interests they share. The characteristic that binds our community is passion—specifically, a passion for hard work. It is inspiring just to be part of it.

In a community like ours, all of the interactions are unrehearsed. Sometimes we don't get everything right. Maybe we use the wrong word or something is off in a gesture or in the way we express ourselves. But these imperfect moments allow for the cross-pollination of ideas. In this way, our beautiful community continues to grow and evolve.

ACKNOWLEDGMENTS

We must first thank everyone who we've been so fortunate to feed: our customers. Your sincere interest, curiosity, and enthusiasm are what inspired us to create this book. It's with gratitude that we can share with you the very experience that so many of you have had a hand in creating.

To all our friends and family at Hartwood: this book could not have been possible without your love and hard work. It's your support that has given foundation to a dream.

Antonio May Balam y familia

Samuel Kanxoc

Raul Flores Ramos

Gabriela Ramos

Valentin Quijas

Viviana Mendez

Manuela Jimenes López

Balo Orozco

Colin Busby

Leticia Ramirez

Walter Hernandez

Roberto Morris

Jose Mariano Ruiz de la Mora

Estefania Sanchez

Erick Moreno

Armando Quijas

David Garcia

Andrea Gallego

Adelsy Avendano

Jesus, Mich, Felix, y Yenisei

Maleny Reyes Osuna

Roberto Herrera

Christian Klamroth Bermudez

Phoot Balam

James Greenfield y Sam

Tommaso Marchiorello

Max de Zambiasi

Jiri Filipek

Orlando Avila

Martin y Luis los Pescadores

Alfredo y familia los Pescadores

Christian Bongiovanni

Juan Taxista

Gulimer Taxista

Palaperos de Macario

Paulina y Lalo

Lina Avila

Merrill Moore

Laura Rodriguez

SPECIAL THANKS TO:

Ann Bramson

Michelle Ishay–Cohen

Renata Di Biase

Nancy Murray

Lelia Mander

Katherine Cowles

Oliver Strand

Christine Muhlke

Andrea Gentl & Martin Hyers

Judith Sutton

Gillian Masland

Alison Roman

Todd Selby

Dulci DeCarlo

Frank DeCarlo

Rémy Robert

René Redzepi

Alice Waters

Elisabeth Prueitt

Chad Robertson

Sam Buffa

Jean Adamson

To Jamie Klotz, thank you for working alongside all of us. You are part of the Hartwood family and we acknowledge your hard work and commitment. *Muchas gracias, amiga.*

ABOUT THE AUTHORS

ERIC WERNER began his training at Payard in New York City and then moved to 71 Clinton Fresh Food. But it was at Peasant and later Vinegar Hill House in Brooklyn that his embrace of the wood-fired cooking methods he'd explored over campfires in his youth found full expression. Together with Mya Henry he owns and operates Hartwood in Tulum, Mexico.

MYA HENRY, along with her co-author and co-owner, conceived, designed, and outfitted Hartwood and is the operational genius behind it. Prior to opening the restaurant, she worked in the restaurant/hospitality industry at the Tribeca and Soho Grand hotels and at The Standard Grill.

CHRISTINE MUHLKE is Executive Editor of *Bon Appétit* and has written books with Eric Ripert and David Kinch.
OLIVER STRAND writes for *The New York Times*, *The Wall Street Journal*, and *Vogue*.

INDEX

CONVERSIONS

WEIGHTS		VOLUME			OVEN TEMPERATURE			
US/UK	METRIC	AMERICAN	IMPERIAL	METRIC		°F	°C	GAS MARK
¼ OZ	7 G	¼ TSP		1.25 ML	VERY COOL	250–275	130–140	½–1
½ OZ	15 G	½ TSP		2.5 ML	COOL	300	148	2
1 OZ	30 G	1 TSP		5 ML	WARM	325	163	3
2 OZ	55 G	½ TBSP (1½ TSP)		7.5 ML	MEDIUM	350	177	4
3 OZ	85 G	1 TBSP (3 TSP)		15 ML	MEDIUM HOT	375–400	190–204	5–6
4 OZ	115 G	¼ CUP (4 TBSP)	2 FL OZ	60 ML	HOT	425	218	7
5 OZ	140 G	1/3 CUP (5 TBSP)	2½ FL OZ	75 ML	VERY HOT	450–475	232–245	8–9
6 OZ	170 G	½ CUP (8 TBSP)	4 FL OZ	125 ML				
7 OZ	200 G	2/3 CUP (10 TBSP)	5 FL OZ	150 ML				
8 OZ (½ LB)	225 G	¾ CUP (12 TBSP)	6 FL OZ	175 ML				
9 OZ	255 G	1 CUP (16 TBSP)	8 FL OZ	250 ML				
10 OZ	285 G	1¼ CUPS	10 FL OZ	300 ML				
11 OZ	310 G	1½ CUPS	12 FL OZ	350 ML				
12 OZ	340 G	1 PINT (2 CUPS)	16 FL OZ	500 ML				
13 OZ	370 G	2½ CUPS	20 FL OZ (1 PINT)	625 ML				
14 OZ	400 G	5 CUPS	40 FL OZ (1 QT)	1.25 L				
15 OZ	425 G							
16 OZ (1 LB)	450 G